POLITICAL PROFILES

MITT ROMNEY

POLITICAL PROFILES

MITT ROMNEY

David Aretha

**MORGAN
REYNOLDS**
P U B L I S H I N G

Greensboro, North Carolina

POLITICAL PROFILES

BARACK OBAMA

AL GORE

HILLARY CLINTON

NANCY PELOSI

ARNOLD SCHWARZENEGGER

TED KENNEDY

MICHELLE OBAMA

JOHN LEWIS

JOE BIDEN

MICHAEL BLOOMBERG

SARAH PALIN

MITT ROMNEY

Political Profiles
Mitt Romney
Copyright © 2013 by Morgan Reynolds Publishing

Morgan Reynolds Publishing, Inc.
620 South Elm Street, Suite 387
Greensboro, NC 27406 USA

ꞵꞵ

Library of Congress Cataloging-in-Publication Data

Aretha, David.
  Political profiles : Mitt Romney / by David Aretha.
      p. cm.
  Includes bibliographical references and index.
  ISBN 978-1-59935-344-9 -- ISBN 978-1-59935-345-6 (ebook)
  1. Romney, Mitt--Juvenile literature. 2. Politicians--United States-
-Biography--Juvenile literature. 3. Presidential candidates--United
States--Biography--Juvenile literature. 4. Governors--Massachusetts--
Biography--Juvenile literature. I. Title. II. Title: Mitt Romney.
  E901.1.R66A74 2013
  974.4'044092--dc23
  [B]

                          2012014189

Printed in the United States of America
First Edition

Book cover and interior designed by:
Ed Morgan, navyblue design studio
Greensboro, NC

TABLE OF CONTENTS

CHAPTER ONE

Young Mitt

Mitt Romney gives his father, George Romney, a hug at a news conference on February 10, 1962, after the auto executive announced he would run for the Republican nomination for governor of Michigan.

Mitt Romney entered the world of politics early. When his father, George Romney, campaigned to get elected governor of Michigan in 1962, fifteen-year-old Mitt was right by his side, working the campaign's switchboard, passing out sodas at kitchen table strategy sessions, selling campaign trinkets to raise money, serving as a copy boy and yard-sign runner, and, after he got his driver's license, serving as chauffeur.

Campaigning seemed natural to Mitt. Manning booths at Michigan's county fairs, he'd shout to passers-by, "You should vote for my father for Governor. You've got to support him. He's going to make things better."

At one rally, Mitt even dressed in Dutch trousers, a hat, and wooden shoes to lead, along with his parents, a parade of "gaily attired street cleaners," some of whom splashed out "soapy water from hickory barrels," to show Michiganders "the sparkling fresh look" the Republican candidate George Romney would bring to the state.

"Young Mitt is eating up the excitement of our new venture," George Romney wrote to relatives in a 1962 letter. He added that Mitt "has had a chance to see some of the wheels go round and he loves it."

Willard Mitt Romney was born in 1947, and his birth came as a surprise to his parents, George and Lenore Romney. After giving birth to Margo Lynn (1935), Jane (1938), and Scott (1941), Lenore Romney had been told by her doctor that problems had developed with her reproductive system, and that she and her husband were done having children.

Yet in 1946, Lenore unexpectedly became pregnant. "I don't see how she became pregnant," her doctor said, "or how she carried the child." Lenore was bedridden for a month. To kill time, she laid on her back, quoting Emily Dickinson poems.

At the time, George Romney was an up-and-coming executive with the Automobile Manufacturers Association. On March 13, 1947, using the Association's letterhead, George Romney announced his son's birth in a letter to relatives.

> DEAR FOLKS,
> WELL, BY NOW MOST OF YOU HAVE HEARD THE REALLY BIG NEWS, BUT FOR THOSE WHO HAVEN'T WILLARD MITT ROMNEY ARRIVED AT TEN AM MARCH 12. . . . A COUPLE OF YEARS AGO, THE DOCTOR TOLD LENORE THAT HER CONDITION WOULD NOT PERMIT HER TO HAVE ANOTHER CHILD AND THAT SHE WOULD HAVE TO UNDERGO A MAJOR OPERATION. HOWEVER, SHE HAD A LOT OF FAITH. . . . WE CONSIDER IT A BLESSING FOR WHICH WE MUST THANK THE CREATOR OF ALL.

Mitt Romney

Lenore Romney called Mitt her "miracle baby."

George and Lenore named the infant Willard Mitt after two remarkably successful men. J. Willard Marriot, who would establish the Marriot hotel chain, was a close friend of George. Milton "Mitt" Romney, George's cousin, had been a starting quarterback with the Chicago Bears in the 1920s.

In his early years, Mitt attended public school in Detroit. In kindergarten, he was known as Billy. But then he heard a song called "Billy Boy," "and it talked about kissing and your mother and so forth," he said. "And I decided that was a terrible song. And I came home and said, 'I can't live with that name any longer.' And I talked with my mom about what name I could use. She said, well, you could use your middle name. And so sometime in kindergarten I switched to Mitt, and I have been on the Mitt name ever since."

When Mitt was seven, George Romney became president and chairman of the board of American Motors, a company on the brink of bankruptcy. Big cars were all the rage in the mid- to late 1950s. But the recession of 1958 inspired George Romney to take a risk on something he called the "the compact car." The unflashy Rambler American proved a huge success. By 1959, the company's stock had skyrocketed to ninety dollars a share from seven dollars, and George Romney was the Rambler's chief pitchman. "Ladies," he'd say at women's clubs, "why do you drive such big cars? You don't need a monster to go to the drugstore for a package of hairpins. Think of the gas bills!"

Political Profiles

Mitt idolized his father, and he seemed to inherit his love for cars. Mitt's brother Scott said he "could always make the great sounds of cars when he was a little kid. . . . I heard him often making the sounds of [squealing tires] around corners."

The family eventually moved to the Detroit suburb of Bloomfield Hills, one of the wealthiest cities in America. However, to counter their life of privilege, George and Lenore Romney sought to instill working-class values in Mitt and his siblings. Each child had assigned chores, including shoveling snow, and George Romney made the children walk where they needed to go. Jane Romney recalled walking a mile and a half to and from her dancing lessons.

By all reports, Mitt had a healthy, happy childhood. Though the baby of the family, his parents tried to make sure he wasn't spoiled. One of his chores was pulling weeds in the garden.

"I hate to weed," Romney wrote years later. "After what seemed like hours of work, I never could see much progress, and I'd complain to my dad. 'Mitt,' he would reply, 'the pursuit of the difficult makes men strong.'"

Romney took that lesson to heart. Throughout his adult years, he would develop a pattern of taking on extraordinarily difficult challenges.

Mitt and his father had an especially close relationship, and Mitt, more so than his older brother and sisters, seemed most able to calm his father's stubbornness and hot temper. "Scott would get upset," said Jane. "I'd get quiet and blow later. My sister would just turn and run. But Mitt talked it through."

An informal family portrait at the home of George and Lenore
Romney in March 1968. Mitt, age fourteen, is standing.

When George Romney would gather the family to
share a new, big idea, for example, Scott recalled
that he and his sisters would say, "Gee, that sounds
fabulous." Mitt's response, on the other hand, was
typically, "Well, have you thought about this?"

This ability to talk and think through situations
most likely came from Lenore Romney, according to
Jane. "My dad would get emotional. Mother wouldn't.
She would be kicking [my father] under the table
to calm him down. And he would say, 'Why are you
kicking me under the table.'"

George and Lenore Romney in 1962

Lenore Romney was a force in her own right. Before marrying George Romney, she had acted on stage and on screen, landing small parts in Hollywood films with stars such as Greta Garbo, and she had worked as a voice actor in animated cartoons. MGM offered the 1929 graduate of George Washington University a three-year $50,000 contract, not long after her arrival in Hollywood. But she gave up her promising career to marry and raise four children.

George Romney never graduated college. "He apprenticed, as a lath and plaster carpenter, and he was darn good at it," Mitt said of his dad. "He learned how to put a handful of nails in his mouth and spit them out, point forward. On his honeymoon, he and Mom drove across the country. Dad sold aluminum paint along the way to pay for gas and hotels."

Unlike George, who was blunt and "terrifyingly earnest," Lenore was reserved, with "a steely will," and she measured her words very carefully. An advocate for women in business and politics, she once remarked, "Why should women have any less say than men about the great decisions facing our nation?"

In years to come, Mitt would exhibit characteristics of both parents—George, his hard-driving father, and Lenore, his gracious, measured mother.

The Romneys' Mexican Roots

By all accounts, the Romneys were fairly typical of families living in suburban Bloomfield Hills. In a 1958 article in the Detroit *Sunday Times*, Lenore Romney talked about the family, describing nightly gatherings around "popcorn," Saturdays spent churning homemade ice cream, and the "exchange of amusing anecdotes about the day's doings."

But there was one thing that likely distinguished the Romneys from most everyone else in Bloomfield Hills: they had deep roots in the Church of Jesus Christ of Latter-day Saints (LDS), commonly known as the Mormon Church. Today, more Mormons live in the U.S. than ever before; still, they make up only 1.7 percent of the total U.S. adult population, according to a 2007 survey by the Pew Research Center's Forum on Religion & Public Life.

Mormonism dates back to 1830, when American Joseph Smith claimed he had visions of an angel who directed him to buried golden tablets. Smith translated these tablets into the *Book of Mormon*, which is considered by Mormons as sacred text, alongside the Bible and two other texts. Smith is considered a prophet to Mormons. They do not believe in a unified Trinity but do believe that God has a physical body.

THE

BOOK OF MORMON:

AN ACCOUNT WRITTEN BY THE HAND OF MOR-MON, UPON PLATES TAKEN FROM THE PLATES OF NEPHI.

Wherefore it is an abridgment of the Record of the People of Nephi; and also of the Lamanites; written to the Lamanites, which are a remnant of the House of Israel; and also to Jew and Gentile; written by way of commandment, and also by the spirit of Prophesy and of Revelation. Written, and sealed up, and hid up unto the LORD, that they might not be destroyed, to come forth by the gift and power of GOD unto the interpretation thereof; sealed by the hand of Moroni, and hid up unto the LORD, to come forth in due time by the way of Gentile; the interpretation thereof by the gift of GOD; an abridgment taken from the Book of Ether.

Also, which is a Record of the People of Jared, which were scattered at the time the LORD confounded the language of the people when they were building a tower to get to Heaven: which is to shew unto the remnant of the House of Israel how great things the LORD hath done for their fathers; and that they may know the covenants of the LORD, that they are not cast off forever; and also to the convincing of the Jew and Gentile that JESUS is the CHRIST, the ETERNAL GOD, manifesting Himself unto all nations. And now if there be fault, it be the mistake of men; wherefore condemn not the things of GOD, that ye may be found spotless at the judgment seat of CHRIST.

BY JOSEPH SMITH, JUNIOR.
AUTHOR AND PROPRIETOR.

PALMYRA:

PRINTED BY E. B. GRANDIN, FOR THE AUTHOR.

1830.

Mormons are also known for their devotion to their church and strong family ties. They believe in abstention from sex outside of marriage, and they discourage vices such as drugs, alcohol, tobacco, and even coffee and tea. Polygamy was allowed within the church until 1890; and until 1978, the LDS banned men of African descent from its priesthood because it taught that black people were inferior and cursed by God.

Lenore Romney came from a prominent Mormon family in Utah, where the largest concentration of Mormons (35 percent) still live today. President Calvin Coolidge had appointed her father to serve on the Federal Radio Commission. George Romney was born and spent his early childhood in Mexico, where the Romneys had fled to escape U.S. anti-polygamy laws.

In 1885, a small group of Mormon settlers set out for Mexico, following passage of the 1882 Edmunds Act, which stripped thousands of polygamists of their ability to vote and other basic citizenship rights. Among the settlers was Miles Park Romney, Mitt's great-grandfather, who had four wives and thirty children. In the States, Miles had been jailed for "unlawful cohabitation."

So Miles bought a dusty plot along the Piedras Verdes River, with the consent of Mexico's then-dictator, General Porfirio Díaz. Initially, the settler community lived out of wagon boxes, but in time they prospered, building irrigation canals along the side of the valley to plant apple orchards. With prosperity came trouble, though. The community had to contend with Apache raiders as well as corrupt Mexican politicians out to confiscate their land and orchards.

George Romney was born in 1907, three years before the outbreak of the Mexican Revolution of 1910. George's father, Gaskell, who had only one wife, was an affluent carpenter with a thriving home-building business in Mexico. But amid the chaos of Mexico's civil war, the Romneys boarded a train and fled back to the United States. The year was 1912; George was five. "I am a member of a religion that is among the most persecuted minority groups in our history," George Romney reflected years later. He described his family and the others who fled Mexico as "the first displaced persons of the twentieth century."

Top photo: George Romney with his mother, Anna Amelia Pratt Romney, Mexico in 1908. Bottom photo: Mitt Romney's grandfather, Gaskell Romr (right), with Gaskell's son and Mitt's father, George Romney (fourth from left), in Colonia Dublan, Chihuahua, Mexico. The Romneys fled by train t U.S. during the Mexican Revolution.

Mitt and Ann Davies, his future wife, on the day of Mitt's senior prom

Beginning in seventh grade, Mitt attended Cranbrook School, a prestigious, private, all-boys college preparatory school on beautiful grounds in Bloomfield Hills. He was not an athlete and, despite a brilliant mind, did not stand out in the classroom. However, he effused positive energy. He joined the pep squad, served as student manager of the ice hockey team, pulled pranks with his pals, went to school dances, and ran cross-country. Mitt ran so hard during one race that, after reaching the finish line, he fell to the ground and passed out.

It was in high school that Mitt also decided how he wanted to style his hair. His father had swept-back black hair, with white at the temples, and Mitt had grown up listening to people talk about the striking profile his father cast. But Mitt liked the look of a man named Edwin Jones, who worked as his father's top aide at the Mormon Church in Detroit. "He had very dark hair," said Mitt, "it was quite shiny, and . . . you could see it in distinct comb lines from front to back."

The Cranbrook boys often mingled with the girls of the nearby Kingswood School. As a senior, Romney dated Lynn Moon, a sophomore. Lynn remembers the day that Mitt and his teenage buddies got a little goofy.

"He and a bunch of friends," she said, "dressed up in very formal clothing and set a formal table in the median strip of Woodward Avenue, the main drag that runs through Detroit. They had somebody, I think, playing the violin as entertainment for the table, and they had a meal right in the middle of the eight-lane road."

"He was just lively," Lynn recalled. "He made you feel good." And, she added, he "was by far the best date that I had in my high school career. He was such fun and such a gentleman."

Another sophomore, Ann Davies, needed a ride home from that party, and Mitt happily obliged. Like Lynn, Ann quickly fell for the tall young gentleman with the strong jaw and beaming smile—who happened to be her governor's son. Mitt was equally smitten with the slender, pretty Ann.

"Clearly, she was beautiful then," Mitt said. "But there was something else that happened very quickly. . . . I didn't want to be anywhere else but with Ann. I wanted to be with her all the time and couldn't imagine being anywhere else besides being with her."

They went to see *The Sound of Music* on their first date. Another time, the couple and their friends used ice blocks to slide down hills at a local golf course at night. "We did that with a bunch of high school friends," Ann recalled, "and got caught and got put in the paddy wagons.

"He was just fun, fun, fun to be with in high school."

At the school prom that year, Mitt proposed to Ann and she accepted. However, they realized that they were too young to get married.

In April 1965, Romney registered with the Selective Service, which was required by law. He also graduated from high school, and the graduation speaker was none other than his father, Michigan governor George Romney. He advised the seventy-six graduating boys to choose their girlfriends wisely, as they

> WILL HAVE MORE TO DO WITH SHAPING YOUR LIFE THAN PROBABLY ANYBODY ELSE . . . . IF THE GIRL YOU'RE INTERESTED IN DOESN'T ASPIRE YOU TO GREATER EFFORT THAN YOU WOULD UNDERTAKE WITHOUT KNOWING HER, THEN YOU'D BETTER LOOK AROUND AND GET ANOTHER.

The year 1965 marked the beginning of the Cultural Revolution. With racial tensions high and the Vietnam War beginning to escalate, many young men and women—especially those who were well educated—were starting to rebel against America's conservative ideals, including "love of country." As police used excessive force to maintain order in black ghettos, and while the U.S. military was beginning Operation Rolling Thunder—a years-long bombing campaign of North Vietnam that would kill more than 100,000 people—many young Americans were becoming disgusted with the American "Establishment" and the traditional "American way."

That summer, Romney enrolled at Stanford University in California, known as the "Harvard of the West." While the campus became more radicalized as the Vietnam War escalated, Mitt remained clean-cut and straight-laced. In fact, in 1966 he participated in a counter-protest against students who were protesting the war. Even during this era of crisis, Romney's patriotism never waned.

While more than 1.7 million young men were drafted for duty in the Vietnam War (with more than 17,000 draftees dying in combat), Romney got deferments because he was in college and because, beginning in July 1966, he was a "minister of religion." That month, Romney went to France to begin a thirty-month Mormon mission, a traditional duty among those of his faith.

Romney's purpose in France was to convert people in the heavily Catholic nation to the Mormon faith. Almost all of the French citizens he talked to were skeptical and resistant, and he wound up converting only two people in two and a half years. "Sutherickin Schatash! It's humiliatin'!" wrote Romney, quoting the cartoon character Sylvester the Cat, in a letter to friends.

Though Romney was greatly frustrated by the rejection, he persistently plugged away. "Despair not," George Romney told his son in a letter, "but if you despair, work on in your despair."

George Romney could have easily given this advice to himself. Now in his third term as governor, he launched a bid to win his party's nomination to run for president, and he was the front-runner, until he made disparaging comments about how the U.S. military leadership had handled the Vietnam War. Romney said that while giving him a tour in Vietnam, generals and the diplomatic corps had given him, in his words, a great "brainwashing," portraying the progress of the war as better than it really was. Conservatives considered Romney's choice of words disrespectful; some questioned his mental state.

Governor Romney talks with troops outside of the chapel of the base camp at Cu Chi, South Vietnam, on Christmas Day in 1967.

Up until then the popular governor had been seen as a visionary and progressive member of the Republican Party. He had stood up for the causes of labor unions, public education, foreign aid, subsidized preschool and summer school, and civil rights, often against the wishes of both his conservative Mormon Church and the right wing of the Republican Party.

Well known for his candor, George Romney once said, "There is no leader who can provide sound leadership on the backs of unsound principles. Principles are more important than men." Against his party's wishes, he led a march down the center of Detroit in solidarity with Martin Luther King over

Governor Romney (left) walks at the head of an anti-discrimination march in a Detroit suburb on June 29, 1963. The governor helped create the state's first civil rights commission.

voting rights for African Americans. And, in 1964 he made headlines by walking out on presidential hopeful Barry Goldwater at the Republican National Convention because of Goldwater's opposition to civil rights. He accused Goldwater of planning a "racist campaign," and in a follow-up letter added, "The rights of some must not be enjoyed by denying the rights of others."

But the "brainwashing" remark was more than his party could take, and it sank his campaign.

Though sheltered in France from the political fallout, Mitt Romney took the sudden turn against his father hard. After all, Mitt idolized George Romney, later describing him as "the person who I keyed my life off of. He was the person who I looked at as being the definition of a successful human being."

George Romney was not shaken by the fallout, though. "Your mother and I are not personally distressed," he wrote to Mitt. "As a matter of fact, we are relieved. We went into this not because we aspired to the office, but simply because we feel that under the circumstances we would not feel right if we did not offer our services. As I have said on many occasions, I aspired, and though I achieved not, I am satisfied."

In France, Mitt learned the language, debated the French about the Vietnam War, and became the assistant to the mission president in Paris. Tragically, he also was involved in a deadly auto accident.

One afternoon in June 1968, Romney was driving church officials in a silver Citroën on a curvy, dangerous road. Headed his way was a Mercedes driven by a Catholic priest. While passing a truck, the priest entered Romney's lane and barreled into his car. "It happened so quickly that, as I recall, there was no braking and no honking, it was like immediate," Romney said. "I remember sort of being hood-to-hood. And then pretty much the next thing I recall was waking up in the hospital."

Romney lost consciousness, while Mission President Duane Anderson—sitting in the passenger seat—was seriously injured. Anderson's wife, Leola, who was sitting between them, died in an ambulance while en route to the hospital. Romney bounced back strong from the tragedy. After a distraught Duane Anderson returned to the United States, Mitt helped direct the mission. "There's nothing like hard work and time to heal the pain and sorrow of a tragic loss," Romney said. "What we do with our time is not for frivolity, but for meaning."

Mitt continued to stay in touch with Ann, who was attending Brigham Young University, a Mormon school in Utah, and had been converted to the Mormon faith by her future father-in-law George Romney.

"Your gal looked lovely as always," George wrote to Mitt in a February 1967 letter. "I sat next to her in church and asked if that ring of yours on her engagement finger meant what it usually means and she said it did."

When Mitt's letters dried up in the summer of 1968 (following his accident), Ann developed a relationship with Kim Cameron, a star on BYU's men's basketball team. Mitt knew that Ann had been dating Cameron and other guys, but when he returned from France in December 1968, she was waiting for him at the airport alongside his family.

Mitt Romney

On the drive home, Mitt and Ann talked together in the back seat of an Oldsmobile Vista Cruiser. "I don't feel like I've ever been away," Mitt told her. "It's the funniest thing. I just feel like I've always been here." Ann felt the same way. "It's like we've always been together," Mitt told her. And then he said, "Do you want to get married?" and she said yes. "I was totally in love with Ann," he said.

Mitt and Ann's marriage announcement did not go over well with Lenore Romney. Mitt was her youngest child, and he had been gone for two and a half years, and now he wouldn't be able to spend much time with her. On March 21, 1969, the fourth anniversary of their first date, Mitt and Ann got married. They honeymooned in Hawaii, and on the following March 21st, Ann gave birth to Taggart "Tagg" Mitt Romney.

Mitt Romney, age twenty-three, with his first son, Tagg. Mitt and Ann would have four more sons: Matt, Josh, Craig, and Ben.

By that time, Mitt and Ann were both attending Brigham Young and living in a basement apartment. When Mitt graduated in 1971, with a degree in English, he delivered a commencement address. Expectations were high for the intelligent, ambitious Romney, whose father was currently serving in President Richard Nixon's cabinet as U.S. Secretary of Housing and Urban Development. George Romney encouraged his son to get a law degree, but Mitt wanted to go to business school. He decided to pursue both at the same time.

George Romney (left) in a cabinet meeting with President Richard Nixon

Romney enrolled in a four-year program run jointly by Harvard Law School and Harvard Business School. Mitt embraced the extraordinary challenge with an intense focus on the tasks at hand. "Mitt's attitude was to work very hard in mastering the materials and not to be diverted by political or social issues that were not relevant to what we were doing," said Mark E. Mazo, a law school study partner. Added classmate Howard Brownstein, Romney was "a pragmatist and a problem solver."

Business School students often worked in study groups. Romney tried to recruit the best students for his study group, and he inevitably emerged as the group's leader. "He and I said, hey, let's handpick some superstars," said classmate Howard Serkin. "He wanted to make straight A's. He wanted our study group to be No. 1." Despite being a father of two boys (Matt was born on October 21, 1971), Romney worked extra hours to be thoroughly prepared. If his partners weren't fully prepared, Serkin said, "he was not afraid of saying: 'You're letting us down. We want to be the best.'"

In 1975, Romney graduated in the top third of his class in Law School and in the top 5 percent of his class in Business School. Mitt was ready for the business world. "He wanted to make money," Serkin said, "he wanted to solve problems."

And financial companies wanted him. Months before he graduated, he accepted a job offer from the Boston Consulting Group. Like his father before him, Mitt Romney was about to take the world by storm.

CHAPTER THREE

A Head
for Business

Mitt Romney at Bain & Company in 1990

In the mid-1970s, business consulting was an emerging field—and the Boston Consulting Group (BCG) ranked among the hottest consulting companies. While BCG turned away tons of young applicants, it recruited the smart, ambitious, superstar candidate from Harvard— Mitt Romney.

"He was an outstanding recruit with exceptional grades, and he was the very charming, smooth, attractive son of a former presidential candidate," said Charles Faris, the man who tapped Romney to work at BCG. "So everybody was bending over backward to get their hands on him."

Romney had options. He passed the bar exam in Michigan in 1975, which allowed him to practice law in his home state. He also was interested in the auto industry. But in the end, he chose the Boston Consulting Group. He wanted to be the CEO of a company someday, and BCG seemed like a great way to learn about how companies were run. Floundering corporations hired BCG to improve their bottom line. BCG's consultants analyzed the companies' financial data and recommended ways to lower costs, improve production, and gain market share.

This line of work was right up Romney's alley, and he gave it all he had, working evenings and weekends and traveling often. "He worked his butt off," said Faris. Romney was such a rising star that the Boston-based Bain & Company, which enjoyed an even greater reputation than BCG did, wooed him in 1977. Romney took the offer, and he soon became immersed in the "Bain way" of business consulting.

Unlike traditional consulting companies, Bain offered more than just recommendations. Its workers performed "strategic audits" for each of their corporate clients, in which they not only examined the company's records and finances but also analyzed the competition and interviewed former employees. Importantly, Bain forged long-term relationships with each client, making sure that its recommendations were properly implemented and the company was achieving its new goals. "The idea that consultancies should not measure themselves by the thickness of their reports, or even the elegance of their writing, but rather by whether or not the report was effectively implemented was an inflection point in the history of consulting," Romney said.

The Monsanto Company, a giant in the chemical industry, was among Romney's first clients. Ralph Willard was Bain's senior partner on the account. But Monsanto officials were so impressed with Romney's research and analyses that they bypassed Willard and worked directly with the young upstart. "Mitt's a very quick study," said

Wheat seeds treated with bacteria like those colonized in this petri dish are nearly immune to wheat take-all, a root-destroying fungal disease. Monsanto is a leading producer of genetically engineered seed.

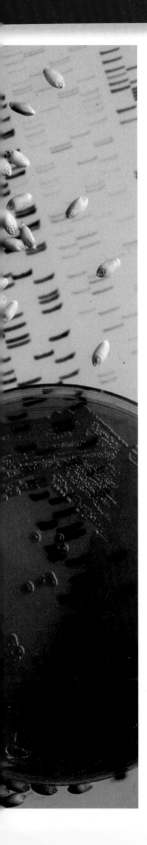

Mitt Romney

Jack Hanley, chief executive of Monsanto at the time. "Every contact we had, I came away impressed."

In 1983, Bill Bain decided to create a spin-off of Bain & Company, called Bain Capital. The chief executive had grown frustrated helping other companies get rich while his company earned only a consulting fee. Bain Capital, he determined, would buy underperforming companies, improve them using Bain techniques, and resell them at a profit, making millions of dollars with each sale. The man he chose to lead Bain Capital: Mitt Romney. Not only did Romney possess the skills for the job, but Bain trusted that he would be a prudent decision-maker. He knew that Mitt wouldn't make reckless decisions that would tarnish the Bain name.

Romney was initially concerned that if the new company failed, he would be out of a job. But Bill Bain assured him that if it did go under, Mitt would get his old job back. So in 1984, Romney, along with Eric Kriss and T. Coleman Andrews III, founded Bain Capital. Romney and his partners hired some of the best and brightest from Bain & Company. "I like smart people, a lot," Romney wrote. "Bill Bain, my old boss, used to joke that most things can be fixed, but smart—or dumb—is forever."

Romney's team spent the first year raising money ($37 million) to invest in other companies. All the while, Mitt kept expenses to a minimum. Office desks were gray metal, not mahogany.

Executives flew coach, not first-class. And although traveling employees could put meals on their expense report, the meals were expected to be "nourishing, but not memorable," Andrews recalled.

Before investing in a company, Romney and his partners analyzed the potential deal in great detail. Romney was extremely careful and cautious, and by 1986 Bain Capital had invested very little. That May, however, they struck gold. Bain Capital invested $650,000 in a new company called Staples, an office supply store, which was the brainchild of former supermarket executive Thomas Stemberg. The first Staples was built in Brighton, Massachusetts, and before long Staples stores began popping up across the country. (Today, there are more than 2,000 Staples in more than two dozen countries.) Bain Capital invested some $2 million altogether in Staples, and after a few years it sold its stake in the company for $13 million.

Staples office supply store

After investing in Staples, Bain Capital focused mostly on leveraged buyouts. In such deals, Bain bought established companies with its capital (that is, its investors' money) combined with borrowed money. If the purchased company failed, Bain Capital's investors and financiers could lose millions of dollars, so *failure* was not an option.

In 1986, Bain Capital (with investor money) bought Accuride, a wheel-making division of Firestone. Using "Bain way" strategies, Romney's team increased Accuride's earnings by 25 percent. When Bain Capital sold its money-making company to Phelps Dodge Corp., it made $120 million—off an original $5 million investment.

When Bain Capital bought a company, it sometimes fired well-paid American employees and outsourced jobs to other companies, where employees worked for low wages. In other cases, Bain Capital simply shut down plants or divisions of companies that were not deemed profitable.

Romney admitted that some jobs were lost in Bain Capital companies, but he claimed that Bain Capital had created thousands more jobs than it had destroyed. The claims were impossible to prove since Bain Capital had not kept track of jobs gained and lost.

Clearly, one company that Romney did improve was Bain Capital itself. The initial $37 million investment fund returned more than $200 million. The acquisition of the Gartner Group (a high-tech research firm), its retooling, and its sale earned Bain Capital an astonishing 1,500 percent return on its investment.

Thomas S. Monaghan, founder and chairman of Domino's Pizza, Inc., (left) and Mitt Romney, managing director of Bain Capital, Inc., sign an agreement for Monaghan to sell a "significant portion" of his stake in the company to Bain Capital in New York.

The *Wall Street Journal* examined seventy-seven investments made by the company under Romney's watch, 1984 to 1999. They found that Bain Capital had generated about $2.5 billion on investments of $1.1 billion, and that the company had posted gains of 50 to 80 percent over the period. Many of the firms that Bain Capital invested in benefited greatly, including Domino's and Sports Authority. But, the *Journal* stated, 22 percent of the companies declared bankruptcy or closed within eight years of Bain's initial investment.

Some of Bain's deals would later tarnish Romney's reputation. In 1988, Bain Capital used high-yield, high-risk "junk" bonds from Drexel Burnham Lambert to finance its purchase of two Texas retail companies. Bain Capital garnered $180 million after investing just $10 million. But when Drexel leader Michael Milken was sentenced to ten years in prison for illegal trading activities, and Drexel went out of business, Romney began to lose his sterling reputation.

In 1989, Bain Capital purchased Damon Corp., and Romney sat on its board of directors. That company would plead guilty to defrauding the federal government; it had billed the government for millions of blood tests that hadn't been necessary. Romney was never implicated in any of the wrongdoing, but Bain Capital wound up earning a threefold return on its investment in Damon. *Blood money*, critics called it.

The story of American Pad & Paper (Ampad) is another blemish. Bain Capital, with a large sum of borrowed money, purchased Ampad in 1992. A year later Ampad's debt was $11 million, and by 1999 that debt had skyrocketed to $400 million. Ampad went bankrupt and hundreds of workers lost their jobs. Despite this disaster, Bain Capital and its investors made more than $100 million on the Ampad deal.

Even though Bain & Company specialized in helping businesses thrive, the company itself was drowning in debt.

So Bill Bain asked Romney to take leave from Bain Capital to help get the Bain & Company ship back on course, and Romney took the job. Soon he was captaining the company out of its sea of red. He began by securing commitments from the company's partners that they would fight this battle with him. They did. Romney then began the turnaround by employing Bain techniques—massive data collection and a strategic audit.

The turnaround took a monumental effort. At first, the financial situation was so bad that the company had to delay payments to suppliers and their landlord (for rent) so that they would have enough money to cut paychecks for their employees. But through wise decision-making and long hours (Romney held planning meetings on Saturdays), Bain & Company turned the corner. In December 1992, with the company thriving once again, Romney returned to his old position at Bain Capital.

In addition to his Herculean efforts in business, Romney devoted up to thirty hours a week to the LDS Church—in addition to the millions of dollars he donated to the LDS. From 1981 to 1986, he served as the church's ward bishop for Belmont, Massachusetts. In that leadership position, Romney met with youth groups, counseled married couples and troubled children, visited the sick, arranged Sunday services and church classes, and used the Bible and the *Book of Mormon* to guide his congregation. From 1986 to 1994, he headed the Boston Stake, which included more than a dozen congregations and some 4,000 LDS members.

CHAPTER FOUR
Olympic-Sized Ambitions

Mitt and Ann address the press in Massachusetts in March 2002

In 1993, Mitt Romney was forty-six years old and questioning his career path. "Do I really want to stay at Bain Capital for the rest of my life?" he asked himself. "Do I want to make it even more successful, make even more money? Why?"

Romney thought of his father, who had said he would have been bored if he had remained in business. "My dad had run for president in 1968 and lost," Romney wrote. "Yet he felt real purpose in the fact that he had spoken out and helped direct the national conversation in ways he thought were important."

That February, he decided to follow the path of his father and run for public office—specifically, a U.S. Senate seat representing Massachusetts. As usual, Romney was incredibly ambitious. If he won the Republican nomination that summer, he would take on incumbent Ted Kennedy, who had held the Senate seat for twenty-five years and had won every one of his reelections in a landslide.

Romney and his campaign "recognized that there was no way I was going to beat" Ted Kennedy. But, he added, "we still felt compelled to try."

Until 1993, Romney had been a political independent. He had funded congressional Democrats, and he had even voted for Massachusetts senator Paul Tsongas in the 1992 Democratic Party presidential primary. But that October, he changed his affiliation to Republican. In the Republican primary for the Massachusetts Senate seat, he faced another businessman, John Lakian, who didn't stand a chance. Spending his own money, Romney advertised heavily on television and won the primary with 82 percent of the vote.

George Romney, now eighty-seven years old, wasted no time taking an active role in Mitt's campaign. He and Lenore even moved into the guest suite above Mitt and Ann's garage. "It was like, 'Oh dear,'" recalled Ann Romney. "We would be just barely getting up, and [George] has already got 10 things he has just got to tell us."

In September 1994, Romney was virtually tied with Ted Kennedy in the polls—a stunning development. The Kennedy family's reputation had been tarnished by the 1991 rape trial of William Kennedy Smith, Ted's nephew. Moreover, American voters were swinging toward Republicans in the 1994 congressional elections. Romney, meanwhile, impressed Massachusetts voters with his business acumen, intelligence, strong family life, and personal charm. His moderate stances on social issues made him palatable to the largely liberal electorate.

Meanwhile, George Romney was counseling his son to loosen up, go off script, speak from the heart, and stop listening to all his consultants. But Mitt remained guarded, more like his mother. Lenore Romney had run for the U.S. Senate in 1970, and Mitt had taken a break from college to help her campaign.

In the end, Lenore Romney took a pummeling in the race. She lost 67 percent to 33 percent. Mitt felt especially bad because of the role he and his brother Scott had played in her campaign. "We were way over our heads and inexperienced," he said, "and offered more ideas than good ideas." What's more, Mitt resented that his mother was not taken seriously as a candidate. Scott recalled that at the start of every debate, his mother's opponent would walk over and hand her a rose.

Lenore Romney later wrote an article for *Look* magazine, in which she talked about the treatment she received as a female candidate. "In factories, I encountered men in small groups, laughing, shouting, 'Get in the kitchen. George needs you there. What do you know about politics?'"

Lenore Romney's treatment and the gaffe that ended George Romney's presidential dreams no doubt cast a shadow over Mitt as he campaigned. "The brainwash thing—has that affected us? You bet," Romney's sister Jane said. "You go, 'OK, can't go there. Don't want to get into that.' . . . Mitt is naturally diplomatic, but I think that made him more so. He's not going to put himself out on a limb. He's more cautious, more scripted."

U.S. senator Edward M. Kennedy (left) and Mitt Romney on stage during a debate at Holyoke Community College in Holyoke, Massachusetts, on October 27, 1994

Kennedy, who had won his previous senatorial elections by 49-, 25-, 40-, 22-, and 31-percent margins, was not fully prepared for Romney's strong challenge. While Mitt spent $7 million of his own money on the campaign, Kennedy spent a hefty $10 million in campaign money and also had to take out a second mortgage on a house. Only after attack ads that highlighted the Ampad disaster—which included interviews with union workers who had suffered—as well as a candidate debate won by Kennedy did the incumbent pull comfortably ahead. Kennedy won the election with 58 percent of the vote to Romney's 41 percent. It was the tightest senatorial victory ever for Kennedy, who would win by 60 and 39 percent in 2000 and 2006.

After the election, Romney did not feel that he had accomplished what he had set out to do, which was "raise new ideas for government, help rebuild a disappearing second party [Republicans], and stand for something bigger than self-interest. We knew all along that we would ultimately lose, but the loss felt worse than we had imagined. For several months, [Ann and I] would say to ourselves, 'Why did we do that?'"

The morning after the election, Romney returned to Bain Capital, where he would remain for another four-plus years. His parents returned to Michigan, and a year later George Romney collapsed while running on a treadmill and died. He was eighty-eight. Three years later, Lenore suffered a stroke and died at age eighty-nine.

In 1998, the Romney family experienced the worst scare of their lives. Ann had been suffering from intense fatigue, numbness on one side of her body, and other symptoms. "It's like a gray cloud that invaded every cell of my body," Ann recalled. "It was in the brain. It was in my muscles. It was in my organs. I had no ability to almost do anything."

That November, she was diagnosed with multiple sclerosis. "I was very, very scared," said Mitt. "I mean, I couldn't operate without Ann. We're a partnership. We've always been a partnership." He took a deep sigh and said, "So her being healthy and our being able to be together is essential."

Ann was treated with corticosteroids and other medications, and her health greatly improved. Instead of continuing with prescription drugs, she turned to alternative medicine: reflexology, accupressure, accupuncture, deep-breathing exercises, and yoga. She also partook in her favorite pastime—horseback riding. Ever since, she has been doing remarkably well for a person with MS. "Whether it's just lucky or whatever, so what?" Mitt said in a 2002 interview. "It's working. So whatever's working, let's keep it going."

In the late 1990s, the U.S. economy boomed like never before, and Bain Capital (and Romney himself) made an enormous amount of money. But as before, Romney wasn't satisfied. "The experience of walking into diners and onto construction sites and hearing people tell me their problems was not easily put aside," he wrote. "I had the bug of wanting to be more involved. I wanted to make more of a difference in people's lives."

Compared to previous years, the American people didn't need Romney's economic advice in 1998. The 4.6 unemployment rate that year was the lowest since 1968, and for the first time since 1969, the federal government had a budget surplus rather than a deficit. Romney found his new challenge that year, but it wasn't in politics, business, or religion. His mission was to save the 2002 Winter Olympics, which would be held in Salt Lake City, Utah.

In January 1999, while on a ski trip in Utah with Ann, Mitt met with Kem Gardner, a Salt Lake City businessman connected to the 2002 Winter Olympic Games. At the time, the Salt Lake City Games were facing a severe crisis. The previous month, the International Olympic Committee had been accused of taking bribes from the Salt Lake Organizing Committee (SLOC) in order to agree to host the 2002 Games, a charge that sparked criminal investigations. The SLOC had just lost their chief executive and needed a new leader, an outsider untarnished by the scandal. Gardner believed the leader should be Romney, who had ties to Utah, was high-profile with a clean reputation, and was famous for his ability to turn organizations around. Gardner introduced Romney to higher-ups involved with the SLOC, and then he talked to Ann, convincing her that Romney was the right man for the job.

Ann believed that Gardner was right, and after numerous discussions with her husband—in which she noted the importance of the Games to Utah and the country, and how he was perfect for the job—Romney agreed to accept the challenge. "My goal is to make Utah proud, make America proud," Romney said in his acceptance speech. "Sure, the managers have messed up big-time, but the athletes haven't, and our job is to go to work for the athletes."

Romney faced enormous challenges, the least of which were accusations that he took the job as a springboard to a political career. The real problems were a $400 million deficit and the SLOC's tarnished reputation. Like he had when he revived Bain & Company, Romney slashed spending and set a tone of frugality. For his first board function as chief executive, he bought pizzas for five dollars, cut them into eight slices, and charged a buck per slice, thus making a three-dollar profit on each pizza.

Olympic Cauldron Park, site of the 2002 Winter Olympic
opening and closing ceremonies in Salt Lake City, Utah

Romney, president of the Salt Lake Organizing Committee, holds the planned Olympic torch during a news conference in February 2001.

More importantly, Romney traveled across the country, reassuring would-be sponsors of the integrity of the Utah Games and convincing them to invest in the Games. According to Fraser Bullock, a former Bain partner and the chief operating and financial officer for the SLOC, Romney helped raise $800 million in sponsorship money.

Despite heavy security due to terrorist fears (the Games took place five months after the 9/11/01 attacks), the 2002 Utah Olympics were universally regarded as a fabulous success. Winter Games records were broken for most tickets sold (1.525 million) and most television viewers (2.1 billion). Moreover, at the conclusion of the Games, the SLOC was tens of millions of dollars in the black.

Mitt Romney

During the Olympics, Romney was both heralded as a savior of the Utah Games and mocked as an egotist. The SLOC produced six official pins featuring Romney. One was a Valentine's Day pin with Romney's head in the center and the words "Hey Mitt . . . We Love You!" in a heart. Another pin pictured him as a heroic figure, with a strong chin and the American flag wrapped around his shoulders.

At the emotional opening ceremonies, Romney stood next to President George W. Bush, whose approval rating at the time was more than 80 percent. To millions on television, it seemed inevitable that Romney—like his father—would become a fixture in Republican politics. Indeed, in the immediate aftermath of the Olympics, Romney was mentioned as a gubernatorial candidate in both Utah and Massachusetts. On St. Patrick's Day, in 2002, as Romney flew to Massachusetts, that state's voters favored him over Republican incumbent governor Jane Swift by a 77 to 12 percent margin, according to a *Boston Herald* poll. When a tearful Swift, whose term had been marred by controversies, announced on March 19 that she would not run, Romney announced his candidacy. He ran unopposed in the Republican primary.

CHAPTER FIVE

Governor of Massachusetts

Governor Mitt Romney answers reporters' questions at the

In the campaign for governor, Massachusetts treasurer Shannon O'Brien gave Romney a run for his money—and Mitt spent lots of it during the campaign, including $6 million of his own fortune. Romney ran as a political outsider who would "clean up the mess on Beacon Hill" and fix the state's budget crisis. To counter his image as a wealthy outsider, Romney rode around on a Boston garbage truck and slung sausages at Fenway Park—all with the cameras rolling, of course. O'Brien slammed her opponent, saying that such efforts were nothing more than a costume party.

O'Brien criticized Romney for his contributions to The Church of Jesus Christ of Latter-day Saints because of its antigay stance. Romney also hurt himself with a TV ad that showed him with his loving family—an ad that made him seem too "perfect" in the eyes of some voters. Nevertheless, Romney overcame all obstacles and won the election with 50 percent of the vote, compared to 45 for O'Brien.

Romney's eventful term as governor, from 2003 to 2007, was marked by a dramatic budget overhaul, groundbreaking health care reform, the "Big Dig" crisis, and other noteworthy events. Despite a state legislature that was predominantly Democrat, the new governor made remarkable progress in several areas, much of which was controversial.

After stocking his cabinet with business and managerial types, Romney took on a budget deficit that exceeded $1 billion. He closed the gap in a variety of ways, including the raising of dozens of fees. "These were not broad-based fees for things like getting your driver's license or your license plate for your car," Romney said, "but instead something like the cost of a sign on the interstate and how much it was going to cost to publish a McDonald's or a Burger King sign on the interstate. We went from, like, $200 a sign to $2,000 a sign."

Actually, many of the fees hit the average taxpayer. For example, he raised the fee for when you buy a house and register the deed with the state. Mike Widmer, president of the Massachusetts Taxpayers Foundation, indicated that Romney went overboard with his fee proposals; he even suggested creating a fee for blind people: ten dollars to receive a state certificate of blindness.

The state legislature, supported by Romney, dramatically cut aid to cities and towns, which helped balance the state's budget but caused grief at the local levels. Cities responded by raising property taxes. After the state reduced funding for higher education, colleges and universities had to jack up tuition.

Romney's greatest budgetary success was the closing of tax loopholes, which helped the state raise hundreds of millions of dollars over the course of his term. In Romney's last two years in office, the state had a budget surplus of around $600 million each year.

An attempt to achieve near-universal health care coverage was the most remarkable aspect of Romney's governorship. A few states had tried to get all, or nearly all, of its citizens covered (Hawaii, Maine, Vermont, Minnesota), but all had fallen short of their goal. Romney began moving toward universal health care soon after he was elected in 2002. "Tom Stemberg, the founder and former CEO of Staples, stopped by my office," Romney recalled. "He told me that 'if you really want to help people, find a way to get everyone health insurance.' I replied that would mean raising taxes and a Clinton-style government takeover of health care. He insisted: 'You can find a way.'"

Romney was also influenced by outside factors. The federal government threatened to cut $385 million in aid to Massachusetts if the number of uninsured people was not reduced. Also, a coalition of health care advocates and religious leaders amassed 112,000 petition signatures to demand insurance for the state's uninsured.

Not having health insurance can be devastating. While emergency rooms are not allowed to turn away sick or injured patients, the bills for such services can be extremely high. Moreover, an uninsured person who needs an operation or incurs a serious disease usually will not be able to afford proper treatment, which could be in the tens or hundreds of thousands of dollars. A 2009 Harvard study determined that 45,000 Americans died each year because they lacked health insurance.

Romney wanted to achieve universal coverage without a government takeover of the state's health care system and without raising taxes. To achieve this seemingly impossible goal, he worked with state legislators (mostly Democrats), U.S. senator Ted Kennedy, insurance companies, business people, academics, hospitals, religious leaders, and advocates for the poor.

On April 12, 2006, Romney signed a bill that was meant to assure near-universal health insurance for Massachusetts residents. The new law would include an individual mandate, a provision that

Romney was adamant about. According to the mandate, individuals above a certain income level were required to obtain health insurance—or else pay an annual fine of up to $1,200. This forced healthy twentysomethings to contribute their fair share to the health insurance pool. Previously, many had refused to because they felt they probably wouldn't need medical care because they were young and healthy.

The new law also included an employer mandate. Companies with eleven or more employees needed to make a "fair and reasonable" contribution toward health insurance or else pay a $295 penalty per employee. Because more health care money would be coming in from these two mandates, the state would subsidize private insurance plans for two purposes: allowing more of the working poor to buy insurance and to expand the number of children who were eligible for free coverage. The law had other progressive provisions, too, such as offering subsidies of up to 15 percent to employees who participated in a wellness program.

"This is probably about as close as you can get to universal," said Paul B. Ginsburg, president of the Center for Studying Health System Change. "They found a way to get to a major expansion of coverage that people could agree on."

Throughout his adulthood, Romney has seemed compelled to take on enormous challenges, and in business he has been remarkably successful. But, critics say, some challenges are too big for Romney to handle, such as the health care system or, perhaps, running the country.

Political Profiles

Romney's record as governor was largely mixed, but he did look like a leader during the "Big Dig" crisis. The Big Dig referred to a massive project in Boston in which Interstate 93 was rerouted into a 3.5-mile tunnel. Due to mismanagement and cronyism within the Massachusetts Turnpike Authority (MTA), the proposed $2.8 billion project would wind up costing more than $14 billion through 2007. Romney wanted to bring the MTA under control of the governor so that he could turn the MTA around, but the state legislature and the courts refused his request. But after three tons of concrete fell on a car that was driving through the tunnel in July 2006, killing Milena Del Valle, the legislature finally agreed to give

The Big Dig in Boston, 2005

the governor some authority. Romney conducted a safety audit, and he forced MTA CEO Matthew Amorello to step down.

Though Romney had run for governor as a relatively progressive Republican, he appeared conservative on social issues during his term. During his campaign in 2002, he was pro-choice in regards to abortion, but in 2005 he switched to pro-life. Throughout his governorship, he fought against same-sex marriage for homosexual couples—a hot-button topic in Massachusetts during those years.

The Massachusetts electorate became less enamored with Romney as his term progressed. His approval rating stood at a healthy 56 percent in January 2005, but that spring, after rumors that he was going to run for president, that number began to drop. On December 14, 2005, thirteen months before his term was over, Romney announced that he would not seek reelection. He spent more than two hundred days in 2006 on the road, strengthening political ties for his presidential run. Many Massachusetts residents felt that he was bailing on them, and his approval rating plummeted to 34 percent in November 2006.

It seemed as if Romney couldn't wait for his next big challenge. On January 3, 2007, one day *before* his governorship ended, Romney established an exploratory committee to raise money for his presidential campaign.

CHAPTER SIX

A Run for President

Romney announced his candidacy
for president at the Henry Ford
Museum on February 13, 2007, in
Dearborn, Michigan.

MITTROMNEY.COM

On February 7, 2007, Mitt Romney journeyed to the Henry Ford Museum outside Detroit to make a big announcement. Inspirational music by John Mellencamp and Neil Diamond blared from the speakers, and a marching band from Divine Child High School contributed to the festivities. Romney, fifty-nine, was flanked by his wife, Ann, their five sons, their five daughters-in-law, and their grandchildren.

"And so," Romney told the gathering, "with them behind us, with the fine people of Michigan before us, and with my sweetheart beside me, I declare my intention to run for president of the United States."

Ann told the crowd, "Every place that Mitt has gone, he has solved problems that people said were nearly impossible." In his campaign, Romney would portray himself as a problem solver and innovator—the one man smart enough and proven enough to fix the ills facing the United States.

Over the next twenty-one months, Republicans and Democrats would wage one of the most hotly contested presidential races in American history. George W. Bush, who was finishing up his second term, had angered many Americans by initiating the seemingly endless Iraq War. The economy was thriving but, many feared, on shaky ground. (Skyrocketing gas prices followed by a collapse in the housing market would lead to a severe economic recession beginning in 2008.) In the Democratic Party, U.S. Senator and former First Lady Hillary Clinton was looking to become the first female president, while charismatic, biracial U.S. Senator Barack Obama was attempting to become the first African American president.

On the Republican side, Romney squared off against a wide variety of candidates. They included John McCain, the tough-as-nails former Vietnam POW who had represented Arizona in the Senate for twenty years. Rudy Giuliani had been a highly successful mayor of New York City and had led New Yorkers through the 9/11 tragedy. The socially conservative Mike Huckabee had served as a Baptist pastor and governor of Arkansas. Ron Paul, a representative from Texas, was a libertarian, meaning he believed in individual liberties and minimizing government's role in society. Former Senator Fred Thompson of Tennessee was perhaps most famous for his acting role on the TV show *Law & Order*.

Romney and former Senator Fred Thompson laugh during the GOP presidential candidate debate in Dearborn, Michigan, on October 9, 2007.

As with Bain Capital and the Utah Olympics, Romney proved adept at raising funds. In fact, he amassed more campaign dollars than any Republican candidate during the primaries—more than $50 million, not including the $35 million of his own fortune that he contributed. But Romney faced a dilemma during the campaign. When he ran for governor of Massachusetts, he had to appeal to the state's largely liberal populace to get elected. But the voters in the 2008 Republican primaries were mostly registered Republicans, meaning he had to seem conservative. His 2008 platform was more conservative than the platform he had when he ran for governor (most notably his switch from pro-choice to pro-life). This elicited charges that he was a "flip-flopper," or someone who changes his stances simply to get elected.

Romney would have plenty of time to discuss his platform during the Republican presidential debates. There would be twenty-one of them, beginning on May 3, 2007, and running through February 2, 2008. During the ninth one, Romney joked about the seemingly endless run of debates, saying it was a lot like *Law & Order*. "It has a huge cast, the series seems to go on forever, and Fred Thompson shows up at the end," he said. Amid the laughter, Thompson replied, "And to think I thought I was going to be the best actor on the stage."

Entering the debates, Romney faced criticism that he was not a true conservative. In the first one, at the Ronald Reagan Presidential Library in Simi Valley, California, Romney tried to denounce that charge. Though President Bush's approval rating was around 35 percent at the time, Romney said he admired Bush's "character, his passion, his love for his country." He also sought to explain why he had "flip-flopped" on his abortion stance. "I've always been personally pro-life, but for me there was a great question about whether or not government should intrude in that decision," he said. He said that the debate over cloning in Massachusetts caused him to change his mind. After the debate, MSNBC political analysts Howard Fineman and Joe Scarborough declared that Romney had won the debate and praised him for the energy he brought to the stage.

According to a poll of viewers by Fox News, Romney won the second debate, in Columbia, South Carolina. But CNN voters put him a distant fourth in the next debate, in Manchester, New Hampshire. In the Des Moines, Iowa, debate on August 6, 2007, Romney took aim at presidential contender Barack Obama, who had talked about taking military action in Pakistan after saying he wanted to have open discussions with the leaders of Venezuela and Iran. "I mean, in one week, he went from saying he's going to sit down, you know, for tea, with our enemies, but then he's going to bomb our allies," Romney said. "I mean, he's gone from Jane Fonda to Dr. Strangelove in one week." (Fonda had visited enemy leaders in North Vietnam during the Vietnam War, and the movie *Dr. Strangelove* parodied bomb-happy American leadership.)

Despite his squeaky-clean image, Romney sometimes fired sharp jabs at his opponents on stage. In a September debate, he accused Giuliani of welcoming illegal aliens to his city when he was mayor. "[I]f you happen to be an undocumented alien, we want you in New York, we'll protect you in New York," Romney mocked. In the same debate, Romney jabbed Fred Thompson for his late entry into the presidential race. "Why the hurry?" Romney quipped. "Why not take some more time off?"

Overall, Romney was competitive on stage. Sometimes he ranked fourth or fifth in the debates, according to polls, but in a pair of January debates he came out on top. The last few debates overlapped with the beginning of the primaries and caucuses, which began on January 3, 2008.

Romney's Mormon faith was an obstacle that he had to overcome. According to a Pew survey, more than a third of Republicans and Republican-leaning independents said that Mormonism was not a Christian religion, even though Mormons insist they are Christian. The vast majority of Republican voters were Christian, and a significant percentage said that the candidate's religion was an important factor in how they voted.

In the first Republican battle, the Iowa caucus on January 3, 2008, Huckabee prevailed in the conservative state with 34 percent of the vote, and Romney finished second with 25 percent. The New Hampshire primary, held five days later, looked to be a fierce battle between McCain, who had won the primary in 2000, and Romney, who had governed the neighboring state. Both candidates had campaigned heavily in New Hampshire. McCain won with 37 percent of the vote compared to Romney's 31 percent. Huckabee was a distant third with 11 percent, and Giuliani—the favorite at one point to win the nomination—finished with just 9 percent.

Also on January 8, Romney won the Wyoming caucus, which did not get much fanfare due to the state's small population. But Romney put a positive spin on his victory and his two runner-up finishes. "There have been three races so far," he told his supporters. "I've gotten two silvers and one gold. Thank you, Wyoming."

A Republican delegate (left) holds up her paddle during the
Republican caucus in Cheyenne, Wyoming, in 2008.

Romney's can-do spirit helped him in his home state of Michigan. At the time, the Great Lakes State had the highest unemployment rate in the nation (7.4 percent), due largely to the Detroit area's shrinking share of the auto industry. The curmudgeonly McCain said that Michigan's lost manufacturing jobs weren't coming back. Romney balked. "I want to bring Michigan back," Romney told Michiganders. "I'm not willing to sit back and say, 'Too bad for Michigan. Too bad for the car industry. Too bad for the people who've lost their jobs; they're gone forever.' That's not the kind of pessimism I think that'll make Michigan strong again. I will not rest, if I'm president of the United States, until Michigan is brought back."

Romney's optimism resonated with the state's voters, who gave Romney a clear victory (39 to 30 percent) over McCain. For Romney, it was the high point of his 2008 campaign. "Tonight marks the beginning of a comeback—a comeback for America," he declared to cheering supporters. "Let's take this campaign to South Carolina and Nevada and Florida and all over the country. Let's take it all the way to the White House."

The Republican race was still wide-open, but Romney rode his Michigan momentum into Nevada. He was not only favored to win the Silver State, which had a large Mormon population, but he won in a landslide, garnering 51 percent of the vote.

Mitt Romney

From there, however, Romney's campaign went south—literally and figuratively. Southern Republicans tended to be more socially conservative than those in other states and more committed to their Christian faith. Romney, the moderate Mormon, finished fourth in South Carolina with just 15 percent of the vote, behind McCain (the winner), Huckabee, and Thompson. Romney finished a solid second in the Florida primary, with 31 percent, but again McCain came out on top, making him the party's clear frontrunner.

Romney won the Maine caucus in a rout on February 1, but anxiety crept into his camp. After the Florida primary, Romney was trailing McCain by double digits in the national polls. On February 5, twenty-one states would hold either Republican primaries or caucuses on "Super Tuesday." Romney traveled nonstop, trying to say that he, and not McCain, had the values that Republican voters cherished. Said Romney, "Across the country, conservatives have come together and they say, 'You know what? We don't want Senator McCain; we want a conservative.'"

But as it turned out, voters *did* want Senator McCain. While the Arizona senator won just nine of the twenty-one states—with Romney taking seven and Huckabee the remaining five—McCain won the three big ones: California, New York, and Illinois. Romney's wins were in moderately populated states (Massachusetts, Minnesota, and Colorado) and sparsely populated ones (Alaska, Montana, North Dakota, and Utah). On the day, McCain won 602 delegates to Romney's 201. Overall, a candidate needed 1,091 delegates to clinch the nomination.

Though it was clear that McCain was now romping to victory, Romney refused to throw in the towel. "We're gonna keep on battling," Romney said that night. "We're gonna go all the way to the convention. We're gonna win this thing, and we're gonna get in the White House."

But this time the words rang hollow. The next day, a Romney advisor admitted that "it is tough to saddle up" this morning. And on February 7, Romney dropped out of the race.

Those who had thought that Romney wasn't conservative enough got an earful of right-wing rhetoric during his concession speech. He talked about raising military spending to face all current and potential enemies, even mentioning the "inevitable military ambitions of China."

Mitt and Ann wave after Romney announced to the Conservative Political Action Conference that he is dropping out of the 2008 presidential race. Later in 2008, Ann would face a challenge. A routine mammogram showed a noninvasive early stage of breast cancer. She had a lumpectomy to remove the affected tissue and went through several weeks of radiation.

He also warned against electing "Barack or Hillary" as the next president. "The opponents of American culture would push the throttle, devising new justifications for judges to depart from the Constitution," he said. "Economic neophytes would layer heavier and heavier burdens on employers and families, slowing our economy and opening the way for foreign competition to further erode our lead."

Sounding like Ronald Reagan, the lionized conservative president (whom he mentioned in this concession speech), Romney said, "It's high time to lower taxes, including corporate taxes, to take a weed-whacker to government regulations, to reform entitlements, and to stand up to the increasingly voracious appetite of the unions in our government!"

Once out of the race, the sixty-year-old Romney had plenty of options—including retirement. But he chose to stay in politics, and his vigor never waned. In April 2008, he formed the Free and Strong America PAC, a political action committee that would raise millions of dollars to promote Republican policies and raise money for other Republican candidates. Romney not only endorsed McCain for president but campaigned on his behalf.

Given that McCain was not an economic expert, many pundits believed he would pick Romney—the financial whiz—as his vice presidential running mate. Had McCain anticipated the nearly catastrophic economic crisis that began in late September 2008, just weeks before the election, he might have indeed selected Romney. But, on August 29, McCain chose Alaska governor Sarah Palin as his running mate. Conservative in her politics, and sporting a dynamic personality, Palin initially pushed McCain ahead in some presidential polls. But her lack of national political experience and her sketchy record as governor eventually made her a liability.

On November 4, 2008, with America facing its worst economic crisis since the Great Depression, Barack Obama won the presidential election with 53 percent of the vote to McCain's 46 percent. Immediately afterward, President-Elect Obama prepared to run the country—and Mitt Romney prepared for the 2012 presidential election.

Barack Obama is sworn in as the forty-fourth president of the United States on January 20, 2009.

CHAPTER SEVEN

Take Two: A Second Bid for President

Romney giving an interview at a rally
in Paradise Valley, Arizona

In June 2009, with the unemployment rate at a staggering 9.5 percent and climbing, conservatives already had their eyes on the 2012 presidential election. But who would run for the Republicans? Of the previous presidential candidates, John McCain was in his seventies and Ron Paul, as a libertarian, was unelectable. Rudy Giuliani and Mike Huckabee were no longer factors, and no other Republicans were emerging as exceptionally strong candidates—except Mitt Romney.

"Are you planning a run for the presidency again in 2012?" David Gregory asked Romney on NBC's *Meet the Press* on June 28, 2009. No one dares announce their candidacy for president three years before the election; they risk becoming stale in the minds of voters, and they become targets of the opposition for way too long.

"Well, that's way beyond my horizon at this point, to think about what's going to happen in 2012," Romney said.

"What . . . what I'm . . . what I'm laying the foundation for is picking up [Republican] seats [in Congress] in 2010," Romney mustered.

But it was pretty obvious that Romney was laying the foundation for a presidential run. According to Politico.com's Jonathan Martin in a June 2009 article, "it's not too much of a stretch to say that [Romney's presidential] campaign never really ended." His Boston-based Free & Strong America PAC was staffed with Romney loyalists and campaign veterans. Moreover, his former staffers and supporters—based in Washington and in early-primary states—remained in regular contact with one another. Together they helped Republicans garner votes in the 2010 congressional elections, but they also served as the infrastructure for Romney's next run for president.

Though Romney laid low in 2009 and 2010, his supporters were excited about his chances. "He's obviously the front-runner," said Mark Salter, a former top aide for John McCain, about Romney's chances to win the Republican nomination. From February 2008 to June 2009, his favorability rating had jumped by ten points and his unfavorable rating had dropped by sixteen points. Though President Obama's approval rating was around 60 percent in June 2009, it would steadily decline as the recession dragged on.

While laying low, Romney wrote a book entitled *No Apology: The Case for American Greatness*, which was released on March 2, 2010. *Time* magazine declared that the book "leaves little doubt that he's spent the time away rebooting his message in preparation for an Oval Office bid." Romney promoted the book with a two-month media blitz, in which he trumpeted his vision for America's future while criticizing the president. In fact, the title of the book mocked what Romney called Obama's "American Apology Tour." He and other Republicans had chastised the president for, in their opinion, apologizing for America's behavior, most notably the aggressiveness in Iraq.

Entering 2011, Romney tried to make it clear that he was a red, white, and blue conservative. He was also the favorite to win the Republican nomination. On January 22, 2011, he won the New Hampshire Straw Poll with 35 percent of the votes. Ron Paul was second with 11 percent, followed by Tim Pawlenty, Sarah Palin, Michele Bachmann, and Jim DeMint.

On April 11, Romney announced at the University of New Hampshire that he had formed an exploratory committee as the first step for running for president. "Believe in America" was his new slogan. On June 2 at an outdoor gathering in Stratham, New Hampshire, Romney formally announced his candidacy. He concluded his well-crafted speech by saying . . .

THESE LAST TWO YEARS HAVE NOT BEEN THE BEST OF TIMES. BUT WHILE WE'VE LOST A COUPLE OF YEARS, WE HAVE NOT LOST OUR WAY. THE PRINCIPLES THAT MADE US A GREAT

NATION AND LEADER OF THE WORLD HAVE
NOT LOST THEIR MEANING. THEY NEVER
WILL. WE KNOW WE CAN BRING THIS COUN-
TRY BACK.

I'M MITT ROMNEY. I BELIEVE IN AMERICA.
AND I'M RUNNING FOR PRESIDENT OF THE
UNITED STATES.

At the time of his announcement, many political pundits believed Romney had a strong chance
of becoming the forty-fifth president of the United
States. So much was in his favor. No other high-
profile Republican was running for president. By
June 2011, Romney had raised $18 million for his
campaign; Ron Paul was second with just $4 million.
Moreover, with the economy still in distress and the
federal budget deficit well over $1 trillion, President
Obama was vulnerable. In a CNN/Opinion Research
Corporation poll released on June 8, 2011, Obama's
approval rating was down to 48 percent and his
disapproval rating was 48 percent. His approval rating would decline toward 40 percent as the year
progressed. Romney was the only proven financial
expert running for president.

For Romney, just winning the Republican nomination would not be a cakewalk, despite the fact
that the $56 million he raised in 2011 far outdis-
tanced his competitors. The problem was that many
Republican voters still had not warmed up to Romney and were desperately hoping that a more traditional (or authentic) conservative would emerge.

Mitt Romney

This desire was reflected in the polling. According to a consensus of polls, Romney had a big lead in the Republican nomination race from January to August 2011. Then came the "flavor of the month" candidates. Texas governor Rick Perry, who many compared to George W. Bush, took a big lead in September. But as his political record was dissected, he began to plummet. In late October, dynamic African American businessman Herman Cain rose to the top of the polls. Multiple allegations of sexual misconduct would bring him down. From late November through the end of the year, former Speaker of the House Newt Gingrich took a big lead. But his numbers would tank in early 2012.

Three contenders in the 2012 race to win the Republican nomination for president

Rick Perry

Herman Cain

Newt Gingrich

From August 2011 to early 2012, Romney was sometimes tops in the polls; when he wasn't, he was *always* second. While others shot to the top and then crashed and burned, Romney consistently garnered 20-some percent of the vote in the polls and sometimes topped 30 percent.

But while he was doing seemingly everything right to get elected, Romney couldn't win over even a third of Republicans. It prompted *Time* magazine to run a cover story on Romney in December entitled "Why Don't They Like Me?" "Romney has problems he can't do anything about," wrote the article's author, Joe Klein. "He's wealthy, a member of the Establishment in a party that is trending very strongly toward right-wing populism. He's also a Mormon, which is rarely mentioned by Republicans, but is an obvious disadvantage among the party's evangelical protestant base. But the biggest problem he has is his persistent flip-floppery. . . . He has never really run as who he actually, well, probably is."

Klein opined that Romney the person was more progressive than Romney the candidate on health care reform and environmental issues. "The radical turn of the Republican party has forced Romney to move right on those and a myriad of other issues," Klein wrote. As a Mormon, Klein stated, Romney was more conservative than even mainstream Republicans when it came to the issues of abortion, gay rights, and premarital sex.

That winter, a joke began making the rounds. "A liberal, a moderate, and a conservative walk into a bar," the joke goes. "Bartender looks up and says, 'Hi, Mitt!'"

Unlike Gingrich and Cain, Mitt Romney at least didn't have any skeletons in his closet . . . except for the story of Seamus, the family dog. Back in 1983, the Romneys took a twelve-hour road trip to their cottage in Ontario, Canada. Seamus rode in a carrier that was secured on the roof of the station wagon. During the trip, the Irish setter began suf-

Seamus, the Romneys' dog

fering from diarrhea, with the excrement rolling down the windows. Mitt washed off the car and the dog at the gas station, then put Seamus back in the carrier for the duration of the trip. The story was retold in a Gingrich TV ad in January 2012, and it did not sit well in a nation filled with dog lovers.

As a front-runner in the 2012 campaign, Romney took a lot of criticism from his opponents during the debates—particularly over "Romneycare." In 2010, President Obama signed health care legislation that was meant to provide coverage for a much greater percentage of Americans. Derisively calling it "Obamacare," Republicans said the legislation was rife with potential problems (particularly costs) and vowed to repeal it. Romney opposed the legislation, too. But, said debate opponent Rick Santorum, a socially conservative U.S. senator from Pennsylvania, "You just don't have credibility . . . your consultants helped Obama craft Obamacare."

Romney replied that the Massachusetts plan "was something crafted for a state. And I've said time and again, Obamacare is bad news. It's unconstitutional, it costs way too much money, a trillion dollars, and if I'm president of the United States, I will repeal it for the American people."

In that same debate, in Las Vegas on October 18, Romney got into a nasty tiff with Texas "tough guy" governor Rick Perry. In what many regarded as a cheap shot, Perry criticized Romney for allowing a lawn service company that employed illegal immigrants to work at his home. "The idea that you stand here before us and talk about that you're strong on immigration is on its face the height of hypocrisy," Perry said. When Romney tried to respond, Perry wouldn't let him answer, prompting Romney to get agitated. The quotes below are just a sampling of their long, stressful back-and-forth with each other.

Romney and Perry during a Republican presidential debate in Las Vegas

PERRY: "THEY WANT TO HEAR YOU SAY THAT
YOU KNEW YOU HAD ILLEGALS WORK-
ING AT YOUR . . ."

ROMNEY: "WOULD YOU PLEASE WAIT? ARE YOU
JUST GOING TO KEEP TALKING?"

PERRY: "YES, SIR."

ROMNEY: "YOU HAVE A PROBLEM WITH ALLOWING
SOMEONE TO FINISH SPEAKING. AND I
SUGGEST THAT IF YOU WANT TO BECOME
PRESIDENT OF THE UNITED STATES, YOU
HAVE GOT TO LET BOTH PEOPLE SPEAK.
SO FIRST, LET ME SPEAK."

Romney hurt himself in the Des Moines, Iowa, debate on December 10. After Perry accused him of deleting a line related to health care reform in a reprint of his book, Romney said he'd bet him $10,000 that he had not done so. Had he bet him five bucks, it wouldn't have been an issue. But in the eyes of some viewers, the $10,000 figure made Romney seem like a wealthy elitist.

Newt Gingrich portrayed Romney as a greedy corporate shark during their important debate in Manchester, New Hampshire, on January 7, just three days before the New Hampshire primary. Gingrich said he was not "enamored of a Wall Street model where you can flip companies, you can go in and have leveraged buyouts, you can basically take out all the money, leaving behind the workers."

Romney had the last laugh in New Hampshire, not only prevailing over Ron Paul by 16 percentage points but quadrupling Gingrich's vote total. But while Romney was riding high after his New Hampshire victory—with polls, pundits, and odds-makers indicating that he was the heavy favorite in the Republican field—a rocky road lay ahead. Republican primary voters would prove to be unpredictable, if not fickle.

Down around 10 percentage points in the polls before the next primary, in South Carolina, Gingrich surged ahead after a pair of strong debates. He won by more than 12 percent over Romney. Considering that it was a Deep South state and heavily Christian, the Romney camp was not concerned. Romney mounted a heavy advertising campaign in Florida, featuring mostly negative ads toward his opponents. Gingrich continued to take jabs at Romney, calling him "some guy who has Swiss bank accounts, Cayman Islands accounts, [and] owns shares of Goldman Sachs that forecloses on Florida."

Romney wound up swinging the pendulum in Florida, amassing 46 percent of the vote. By that point, only Gingrich (32 percent in Florida), Santorum (13 percent), and Paul (7 percent) remained in the race. As in previous primaries, many exit poll respondents said they voted for Romney because they felt he had the best chance of beating President Obama in the general election. After Romney breezed in the Nevada caucus on February 4, garnering 50 percent of the vote, some odds-makers tabbed him as a 20-1 favorite to win the nomination. But then everything changed.

First of all, nasty advertisements were tarnishing both Romney and Gingrich. Through early February 2012, according to the *Washington Post*, the percentage of negative ads in the Republican primary had risen from 6 percent in 2008 to nearly 50 percent. While those familiar foes duked it out, Santorum campaigned hard in Minnesota, Missouri, and Colorado, all of which held primaries on February 7. Santorum's wins in the first two states were impressive, but his triumph in Colorado stunned the nation and rocked the Romney camp. Not only had Romney won Colorado in 2008, but a poll conducted on February 4 had him ahead by 14 percentage points. "Conservativism is alive and well," declared a victorious Santorum.

Romney's odds of winning dropped from 20-1 to
3-1, as Santorum was on his heels. Michigan was the
next primary, on February 28, and polls had the two
new rivals neck-and-neck in Romney's home state.
Romney blundered badly when he declared that
President Obama should not have bailed out General
Motors and Chrysler when they went broke several
years earlier. Romney insisted that private industry
should have provided the money for their restruc-
turing—not the federal government. That did not
sit well among many Michigan residents, since the
Detroit automakers had flourished since the bailout.
Besides, no private companies had been willing to
invest in GM or Chrysler.

Picketers outside of the Republican presidential debate at Oakland
University in Auburn Hills, Michigan. Romney had earlier suggested
that auto companies should be allowed to go bankrupt.

When Romney delivered a major economic speech in Detroit, it was overshadowed by a verbal gaffe. Trying to show that his family drove Detroit-made automobiles, he said that his wife drove a couple of Cadillacs. Once again, this came out as an elitist statement. Cadillacs are luxury cars that have long been associated with the wealthy—and Ann had two of them.

Romney ended up winning the Michigan primary with 41 percent of the vote compared to Santorum's 38 percent. Next up was Super Tuesday on March 6, with ten states up for grabs. On the surface, it seemed like a great day for Romney. While Gingrich won his home state of Georgia—and Santorum prevailed in the conservative states of Oklahoma, Tennessee, and North Dakota—Romney prevailed in six states. He took Massachusetts, Virginia, Vermont, Idaho, Alaska, and Ohio.

The Ohio victory was especially sweet, since polls had indicated that it could go either way—Romney or Santorum. Romney trailed in Ohio much of the night before winning by less than 1 percent. By the next morning, Romney had a large lead in the Republican delegate count. He had amassed 415 delegates, well ahead of Santorum (176), Gingrich (105), and Paul (47). A total of 1,144 delegates were needed to win the nomination.

Still, Romney could not breathe easy. The press noted how Santorum was not fading away like all of Romney's previous challengers. They pointed out that Romney had barely won Ohio despite outspending Santorum twelve to one in that state. A poll revealed that Romney's approval rating among Independent voters was an alarmingly low 29 percent—and his disapproval rating among them was 44 percent. Moreover, he could not shake the "elitist" label. On one liberal talk show, the host played a trivia game with his callers: "Who Said It: Mitt Romney or Mr. Burns?" The latter referred to the out-of-touch tycoon on *The Simpsons*.

If that wasn't enough, Romney next faced ridicule and questioning after a longtime aide, during a CNN interview, used the children's toy Etch-A-Sketch to describe how Romney would change his views and tactics during a fall match-up with President Obama. Romney has been persistently dogged and widely criticized for his contradictory positions. The aide's remarks conjured up fears that, truth be known, Romney had no core political philosophy; or, if he did, no one knew for sure what it was.

In that way, Mitt Romney could not be more different than his father. George Romney was a straight-talker, whose "shocking authenticity" and "courage in sticking to his positions without fear or favor" were his "calling card," political commentators Rick Perlstein and Michael Tomasky wrote in an article for *The American Prospect*. George Romney refused to bend for the sake of political expediency, whether during his time as governor of Michigan or during his short-lived bid to win the White House.

"I can't change myself to fit what people want," he once told an interviewer. "I'm not a political animal in that sense."

Mitt Romney's campaign forged full-steam ahead, in spite of all the slings and arrows thrown his way. In April, Romney cemented his status as the GOP front-runner, after his top challenger, Rick Santorum, suspended his campaign. Then in May he won the Texas primary, putting him above the 1,144 delegates required to clinch the party's nomination. After the Texas win, Romney said in a statement:

> I AM HONORED THAT AMERICANS ACROSS THE COUNTRY HAVE GIVEN THEIR SUPPORT TO MY CANDIDACY AND I AM HUMBLED TO HAVE WON ENOUGH DELEGATES TO BECOME THE REPUBLICAN PARTY'S 2012 PRESIDENTIAL NOMINEE. OUR PARTY HAS COME TOGETHER WITH THE GOAL OF PUTTING THE FAILURES OF THE LAST THREE AND A HALF YEARS BEHIND US. I HAVE NO ILLUSIONS ABOUT THE DIFFICULTIES OF THE TASK BEFORE US. BUT WHATEVER CHALLENGES LIE AHEAD, WE WILL SETTLE FOR NOTHING LESS THAN GETTING AMERICA BACK ON THE PATH TO FULL EMPLOYMENT AND PROSPERITY.

Ahead for Romney would be nothing but tremendous challenges: months of day-and-night campaigning, relentless media scrutiny, and, if he beat Barack Obama in November 2012, the job of presiding over a nation with a $1.3 trillion budget deficit and an endless list of astronomical problems.

Could one person turn America around? That's highly doubtful. But one man truly *believed* he could. His name: Mitt Romney.

Mitt Romney with his wife, Ann, and three of their five sons: (from left to right) Craig, Josh, and Matt

Timeline

1947: Born Willard Mitt Romney on March 12 in Detroit, Michigan, the fourth and last child of George W. Romney, an automobile executive, and his wife, Lenore.

1962: Helps his father, George, campaign for governor of Michigan; father wins.

1965: Graduates from Cranbrook School in Bloomfield Hills, Michigan; enrolls at Stanford University.

1966: Completes second semester at Stanford; begins a thirty-month Mormon mission in France.

1967: Father, George, announces candidacy for president; withdraws from the campaign a few months later.

1968: Survives a car crash in which the wife of a fellow Mormon missionary dies; finishes mission in France.

1969: Marries high school sweetheart Ann Davies on March 21, 1969; father serves as secretary of housing and urban development during President Richard Nixon's first term.

1970: First of five sons, Taggart, is born; works on mother's U.S. Senate race in Michigan.

1971: Graduates from Brigham Young University with a degree in English.

1975: Graduates with business and law degrees from Harvard University; joins the Boston Consulting Group.

1977: Joins the Bain & Company consulting firm; quickly earns a reputation as a rising star.

1984: Co-founds Bain Capital; amasses a personal fortune during his fifteen years running the highly successful investment company.

1986 to 1994: Heads the Boston Stake, which includes more than a dozen congregations of The Church of Jesus Christ of Latter-day Saints.

1994: Loses to Ted Kennedy in the election for a Massachusetts Senate seat.

1998: Wife, Ann, diagnosed with multiple sclerosis.

1999: Serves as president and CEO of the 2002 Salt Lake City Olympic Games Organizing Committee from 1999 to 2002.

2002: Elected governor of the Commonwealth of Massachusetts.

2006: Signs into a law legislation requiring Massachusetts citizens to have health insurance.

2007: Announces that he is running for president.

2008: Drops out of the presidential race after John McCain virtually secured the Republican nomination on Super Tuesday; endorses McCain.

2010: Release of his book, *No Apology: The Case for American Greatness*.

2011: Announces that he is running for president.

2012: Wins the Texas primary in May, putting him above the 1,144 delegates required to clinch the GOP nomination.

Sources

Chapter One: Young Mitt

p. 11,   "You should vote . . ." Karen Tumulty, "What Romney Believes," *Time* (International: Canada Edition), May 21, 2007, http://www. time.com/time/magazine/article/0,9171,1619536,00.html.

p. 11,   "gaily attired . . ." Maeve Reston, "Mitt Romney Grew Up on Politics," *Los Angeles Times*, February 25, 2012.

p. 11,   "Young Mitt . . ." Ibid.

p. 12,   "I don't see how . . ." Neil Swidey and Michael Paulson, "Privilege, Tragedy, and a Young Leader," *Boston Globe*, June 24, 2007, http://www.boston.com/news/nation/articles/2007/06/24/ privilege_tragedy_and_a_young_leader/?page=2.

p. 12,   "Dear Folks . . ." Ibid.

p. 13,   "miracle baby," Ibid.

p. 13,   "and it talked . . ." "Conversations/Live Q&A," *Washington Post*, January 20, 2012, http://live.washingtonpost.com/fact-checker:- south-carolina-debate-120120.html.

p. 13,   "Ladies, why do you . . ." Tumulty, "What Romney Believes."

p. 14,   "could always make . . ." "Erin Burnett Outfront," CNN, January 9, 2012, http://transcripts.cnn.com/TRANSCRIPTS/1201/09/ebo.01.html.

p. 14,   ""I hate to . . ." Mitt Romney, *No Apology: The Case for American Greatness* (New York: St. Martin's Press, 2010), 5.

p. 14,   "Scott would get upset . . ." Neil Swidey, "The Lessons of the Father," *Boston Globe*, August 13, 2006.

p. 15,   "Gee that sounds . . ." Swidey and Paulson, "Privilege, Tragedy, and a Young Leader."

p. 15,   "My dad would get . . ." Swidey, "The Lessons of the Father."

p. 17,   "He apprenticed, as . . ." "Romney's New Message: I Care," Daily Kos, February 9, 2012, http://www.dailykos.com/ story/2012/02/09/1063244/-Romney-s-New-Message-I-Care.

p. 17,   "terrifyingly earnest," A. H. Raskin, "A Maverick Starts a New Crusade," *New York Times Magazine*, February 28, 1960.

p. 17,   "steely will," Sheryl Gay Stolberg, "Political Lessons, From a Mother's Losing Run," *New York Times*, February 23, 2012.

p. 17,   "Why should women . . ." Ibid.

p. 18,   "popcorn . . . days doings," Reston, "Mitt Romney Grew Up on Politics."

p. 20,   "I am a member . . ." Noam Scheiber, "The Inheritance," *The New Republic*, February 16, 2012.

p. 20,   "the first displaced persons . . ." Ibid.

Chapter Two: The Governor's Son

p. 23,   "He had very dark ..." Swidey and Paulson, "Privilege, Tragedy, and a Young Leader."

p. 24,   "He and a bunch ..." Hugh Hewitt, *A Mormon in the White House: 10 Things Every American Should Know About Mitt Romney* (Washington: Regnery Publishing, 2007), 77.

p. 24,   "He was just ..." Ibid., 76.

p. 24,   "Clearly, she was ..." "Spouses," 2012 Presidential Candidates, http://2012.presidential-candidates.org/Spouses.php.

pp. 24-25, "We did that with ..." Steve LeBlanc, "Fortunate Son: Mitt Romney's Life is His Father's Legacy," *Deseret News*, December 16, 2007.

p. 25,   "He was just fun ..." Ibid.

p. 25,   "will have more ..." Swidey and Paulson, "Privilege, Tragedy, and a Young Leader."

p. 26,   "Suthericken Schatash! ..." David D. Kirkpatrick, "Romney, Searching and Earnest, Set His Path in the '60s," *New York Times*, November 15, 2007.

p. 26,   "Despair not ..." Ibid.

p. 27,   "brainwashing," LeBlanc, "Fortunate Son: Mitt Romney's Life is His Father's Leagacy."

p. 28,   "There is no leader ..." Michael Kranish and Scott Helman, *The Real Romney* (New York: HarperCollins Publishers, 2012), 6.

p. 29,   "racist campaign," Kirkpatrick, "Romney, Searching and Earnest, Set His Path in the '60s."

p. 29,   "The rights of some ..." Swidey and Paulson, "Privilege, Tragedy, and a Young Leader."

p. 29,   "the person who I keyed ..." Swidey, "The Lessons of the Father."

p. 29,   "Your mother and I ..." Tumulty, "What Romney Believes."

p. 30,   "It happened so quickly ..." Swidey and Paulson, "Privilege, Tragedy, and a Young Leader."

p. 30,   "There's nothing like ..." Ibid.

p. 30,   "Your gal looked lovely ..." David D. Kirkpatrick, "For Romney, A Course Set Long Ago," *New York Times*, December 18, 2007, http:www.nytimes.com/2007/12/18/us/politics/18romney.html?.

p. 31,   "I don't feel like ..." Hewitt, *A Mormon in the White House*, 80.

p. 32,   "Mitt's attitude was ..." Jodi Kantor, "At Harvard, a Master's in Problem Solving," *New York Times*, December 24, 2011, http://www.nytimes.com/2011/12/25/us/politics/how-harvard-shaped-mitt-romney.html?_r=1&pagewanted=all.

p. 32,   "a pragmatist and a problem solver ..." Ibid.

p. 33,   "He and I said …" Ibid.

p. 33,   "he was not …" Ibid.

p. 33,   "He wanted to …" Ibid.

Chapter Three: A Head for Business

p. 35,   "He was an …" Kranish and Helman, *The Real Romney*, 97.

p. 36,   "He worked his …" Ibid.

p. 36,   "The idea that …" Hewitt, *A Mormon in the White House*, 49.

pp. 36-37, "Mitt's a very …" Robert Gavin and Sacha Pfeiffer, "Plenty of 'Pitting' Preceded Romney's Profits," *Deseret News*, from *Boston Globe*, July 3, 2007, http://www.deseretnews.com/article/680195957/Plenty-of-pitting-preceded-Romneys-profits.html?pg=3.

p. 37,   "I like smart …" Mitt Romney, *Turnaround: Crisis, Leadership, and the Olympic Games* (Washington: Regnery Publishing, 2007), 63.

p. 38,   "nourishing, but not …" Gavin and Pfeiffer, "Plenty of 'Pitting' Preceded Romney's Profits." *Deseret News*, from *Boston Globe*, July 3, 2007, http://www.deseretnews.com/article/680195957/Plenty-of-pitting-preceded-Romneys-profits.html?pg=4.

Chapter Four: Olympic-Sized Ambitions

p. 45,   "Do I really …" Romney, *Turnaround*, 14.

p. 45,   "My dad had …" Ibid.

p. 46,   "recognized that there …" Ibid.

p. 46,   "It was like …" Kirkpatrick, "For Romney, A Course Set Long Ago."

p. 47,   "We were way over …" Reston, "Mitt Romney Grew Up on Politics."

p. 47,   "In factories, I encountered …" Stolberg, "Political Lessons, From a Mother's Losing Run."

p. 47,   "The brainwash thing …" Swidey, "The Lessons of the Father."

p. 49,   "raise new ideas …" Romney, *Turnaround*, 15.

p. 49,   "It's like a …" Jill Radsken, "Ann Romney on Her Choices, Family, Health and Future," All About Multiple Sclerosis, from *Boston Herald*, December 8, 2002, http://www.mult-sclerosis.org/news/Dec2002/AnnRomney.html.

p. 49,   "I was very …" Ibid.

p. 50,   "Whether it's just …" Ibid.

p. 50,   "The experience of …" Romney, *Turnaround*, 16.

p. 51,   "My goal is . . ." Howard Berkes, "Romney's Olympic Legacy: Savior Or Self-Promoter?" NPR, January 13, 2012, http://www.npr.org/2012/01/13/145190620/a-look-at-romneys-olympic-legacy.

Chapter Five: Governor of Massachusetts

p. 57,   "clean up the . . ." John McElhenny, "Romney Sweeps to Victory," Boston.com, November 5, 2002, http://boston.com/news/daily/05/mass_gov.htm.

p. 58,   "These were not . . ." Chris Arnold, "As Governor, Romney Balanced Budget By Hiking Fees," NPR, December 14, 2011, http://www.npr.org/2011/12/14/143657615/as-governor-romney-balanced-budget-by-hiking-fees.

pp. 59-60, "Tom Stemberg, the . . ." Avik Roy, "What Mitt Romney Said About Romneycare When He Signed It into Law," *Forbes*, May 12, 2011, http://www.forbes.com/sites/aroy/2011/05/12/what-mitt-romney-said-about-romneycare-when-he-signed-it-into-law/.

p. 61,   "This is probably . . ." Pam Belluck, "Massachusetts Set to Offer Universal Health Insurance," *New York Times,* April 4, 2006, http://www.nytimes.com/2006/04/04/us/04cnd-mass.html.

Chapter Six: A Run for President

p. 65,   "And so, with . . ." Scott Helman and Andrew Ryan, "Romney Formally Announces Run for President," Boston.com, February 13, 2007, http://www.boston.com/news/globe/city_region/breaking_news/2007/02/romney_formally_2.html.

p. 65,   "Every place that . . ." Ibid.

p. 68,   "It has a . . ." "Romney, Giuliani Spar During Thompson's Debate Debut," CNN, October 9, 2007, http://articles.cnn.com/2007-10-09/politics/thompson.debate_1_debate-debut-mitt-romney-watch-giuliani?_s=PM:POLITICS.

p. 68,   "character, his passion . . ." Adam Nagourney and Marc Santora, "Republican Candidates Hold First Debate, Differing on Defining Party's Future," *New York Times*, May 4, 2007, http://query.nytimes.com/gst/fullpage.html?res=9C07EFDB113EF937A35756C0A9619C8B63&pagewanted=all.

p. 68,   "I've always been . . ." Ibid.

p. 69,   "I mean, in . . ." "Debate's 'Brightest Moment'?" Media Matters for America, August 6, 2007, http://mediamatters.org/mobile/research/200708060007.

| p. 69, | "[I]f you happen . . ." Michael Luo and Michael Cooper, "Republican Candidates Put Bite Into a Debate, With Thompson a Target," *New York Times*, September 6, 2007, http://www.nytimes.com/2007/09/06/us/politics/06debate.html. |

p. 69,   "Why the hurry . . ." Ibid.

p. 70,   "There have been . . ." "Romney Second in N.H., but Pledges Long Fight," MSNBC, January 8, 2008, http://www.msnbc.msn.com/id/22563145/ns/politics-decision_08/t/romney-second-nh-pledges-long-fight/#.Tzf7VSPEOgs.

p. 72,   "I want to . . ." "GOP Candidates Try to Ease Fears, Win Votes in Michigan," CNN, January 14, 2008, http://articles.cnn.com/2008-01-14/politics/michigan.primary_1_michigan-romney-campaign-mitt-romney?_s=PM:POLITICS.

p. 72,   "Tonight marks the . . ." "Romney's Michigan Win Shakes up GOP Race," CNN, January 15, 2008, http://articles.cnn.com/2008-01-15/politics/michigan.primary_1_mike-huckabee-john-mccain-giuliani-campaign?_s=PM:POLITICS.

p. 73,   "Across the country . . ." Eric Weiner, "GOP: McCain Leads Race for Delegates," NPR, February 6, 2008, http://www.npr.org/templates/story/story.php?storyId=18718573.

p. 74,   "We're gonna keep . . ." Scott Conroy, "Romney: 'This Campaign's Going On,'" CBS News, February 5, 2008, http://www.cbsnews.com/8301-502443_162-3796188-502443.html.

p. 74,   "it is tough . . ." Brian Montopoli, "Following Disappointing Super Tuesday, Romney Considers His Options," CBS News, February 6, 2008, http://www.cbsnews.com/8301-502163_162-3798447-502163.html.

p. 74,   "inevitable military ambitions . . ." "Governor Romney's Address To CPAC," Human Events, February 7, 2008, http://www.humanevents.com/article.php?id=24893.

p. 76,   "The opponents of . . ." Ibid.

p. 76,   ""It's high time . . ." Ibid.

Chapter Seven: Take Two: A Second Bid for President

pp. 79-80, "Are you planning . . ." "Meet the Press' transcript for June 28, 2009," MSNBC, http://www.msnbc.msn.com/id/31584983/ns/meet_the_press/t/meet-press-transcript-june/#.Tz0XXyPEOgs.

p. 80,   "it's not too . . ." Jonathan Martin, "Mitt Romney's Team Awaits 2012," Politico, June 29, 2009, http://www.politico.com/news/stories/0609/24316.html.

p. 80,   "He's obviously the . . ." Ibid.

pp. 80-81, "leaves little doubt ..." Alex Altman, "Mitt Romney's No Apology," *Time*, March 3, 2010, http://www.time.com/time/politics/article/0,8599,1969266,00.html#ixzz1mePYsPoo.

pp. 80-82, "These last two ..." "What Romney Said in Stratham," *Concord Monitor*, June 2, 2011, http://www.concordmonitor.com/blogentry/260625/what-romney-said-in-stratham?SESS9834b15542a6fac108 5e8e8200c5ec0c=google.

p. 84, "Romney has problems ..." Joe Klein, "Why Don't They Like Mitt?" *Time*, December 1, 2011, http://swampland.time.com/2011/12/01/ mitt-romney-why-dont-they-like-him/#ixzz1mq34Pps8.

p. 84, "The radical turn ..." Ibid.

p. 85, "A liberal, a ..." "A Liberal, a Moderate and a Conservative Walk into a Bar," Sleepless in Midland, February 10, 2012, http://sleepless. blogs.com/george/2012/02/a-liberal-a-moderate-and-a-conservative-walk-into-a-bar.html.

p. 86, "You just don't ..." "Romney Takes Heat For RomneyCare From Santorum, Gingrich," Real Clear Politics, October 18, 2011, http:// www.realclearpolitics.com/video/2011/10/18/romney_takes_heat_ for_romneycare_by_santorum_gingrich.html.

p. 86, "was something crafted ..." Ibid.

p. 86, "The idea that ..." "Gloves Come Off, Candidates Go All Out in Las Vegas Debate," CNN, October 18, 2011, http://articles.cnn. com/2011-10-18/politics/politics_las-vegas-debate_1_eric-fehrn-strom-romney-and-perry-illegal-immigrants?_s=PM:POLITICS.

p. 88, "enamored of a ..." Dan Primack, "Newt Gingrich's Private Equity Past," CNNMoney, January 9, 2012, htpp://www.finance.fortune.cnn. com/2012/01/09/newt-gingrichs-private-equity-past/.

p. 89, "some guy who ..." Karen Tumulty, "Mitt Romney Florida Primary Win Puts Renewed Pressure on Gingrich," *Washington Post*, February 1, 2012, http://www.washingtonpost.com/politics/ mitt-romney-florida-primary-win-puts-renewed-pressure-on-gin-grich/2012/02/01/gIQA4KO9hQ_story.html.

p. 92, "shocking authenticity ... fear or favor ... calling card," Paul Waldman, "Mitt Romney's Daddy Issues," *The American Prospect*, February 3, 2012, http://prospect.org/article/mitt-romneys-daddy-issues.

p. 93, "I can't change myself ..." T. George Harris, *Romney's Way: A Man and An Idea* (Englewood Cliffs, NJ: Prentice-Hall, Inc., 1967), 195.

p. 93, "I am honored ..." Associated Press, "Mitt Romney Wins Texas Primary," NPR, May 29, 2012, http://www.npr. org/2012/05/29/153956134/mitt-romney-wins-texas-primary" http://www.npr.org/2012/05/29/153956134/ mitt-romney-wins-texas-primary.

Bibliography

Altman, Alex. "Mitt Romney's No Apology." *Time,* March 3, 2010. http://www.time.com/time/politics/article/0,8599,1969266,00.html#ixzz1mePYsPoo.

"An American Century." MittRomney.com. http://www.mittromney.com/collection/foreign-policy.

Arnold, Chris. "As Governor, Romney Balanced Budget By Hiking Fees." NPR, December 14, 2011. http://www.npr.org/2011/12/14/143657615/as-governor-romney-balanced-budget-by-hiking-fees.

Becker, Deborah. "Romney's Jobs Record As Governor Is Up For Debate." Massachusetts High Technology Council, December 15, 2011. http://www.mhtc.org/articles/news/RomneysJobsRecordAsGovUpforDebate.asp.

Belluck, Pam. "Massachusetts Set to Offer Universal Health Insurance." *New York Times,* April 4, 2006. http://www.nytimes.com/2006/04/04/us/04cnd-mass.html.

Berkes, Howard. "Romney's Olympic Legacy: Savior Or Self-Promoter?" NPR, January 13, 2012. http://www.npr.org/2012/01/13/145190620/a-look-at-romneys-olympic-legacy.

Capehart, Jonathan. "Angry Rick Santorum 'throws up' on JFK." *Washington Post*, February 27, 2012. http://www.washingtonpost.com/blogs/post-partisan/post/angry-rick-santorum-throws-up-on-jfk/2011/03/04/gIQA4tiidR_blog.html.

"China & East Asia." MittRomney.com. http://www.mittromney.com/issues/china-east-asia.

Conroy, Scott. "Romney: 'This Campaign's Going On.'" CBS News, February 5, 2008. http://www.cbsnews.com/8301-502443_162-3796188-502443.html.

"Conversations/Live Q&A." *Washington Post,* January 20, 2012. http://live.washingtonpost.com/fact-checker:-south-carolina-debate-120120.html.

"C-Span Transcript, Brian Lamb, Host." Myclob's Mitt Romney Encyclopedia. http://myclob.pbworks.com/w/page/21956982/Brian%20Lamb.

"Debate's 'brightest moment'?" Media Matters for America, August 6, 2007. http://mediamatters.org/mobile/research/200708060007.

"Erin Burnett Outfront." CNN, January 9, 2012. http://transcripts.cnn.com/TRANSCRIPTS/1201/09/ebo.01.html.

Gavin, Robert and Sacha Pfeiffer. "Plenty of 'Pitting' Preceded Romney's Profits." *Deseret News*, from *Boston Globe,* July 3, 2007. http://www.deseretnews.com/article/680195957/Plenty-of-pitting-preceded-Romneys-profits.html?pg=3.

"Gloves Come Off, Candidates Go All Out in Las Vegas Debate." CNN, October 18, 2011. http://articles.cnn.com/2011-10-18/politics/politics_las-vegas-debate_1_eric-fehrnstrom-romney-and-perry-illegal-immigrants?_s=PM:POLITICS.

"GOP Candidates Try to Ease Fears, Win Votes in Michigan." CNN, January 14, 2008. http://articles.cnn.com/2008-01-14/politics/michigan.primary_1_michigan-romney-campaign-mitt-romney?_s=PM:POLITICS.

"Governor Romney's Address To CPAC." Human Events, February 7, 2008. http://www.humanevents.com/article.php?id=24893.

Helman, Scott and Andrew Ryan. "Romney Formally Announces Run for President." Boston.com, February 13, 2007. http://www.boston.com/news/globe/city_region/breaking_news/2007/02/romney_formally_2.html.

Hewitt, Hugh. *A Mormon in the White House: 10 Things Every American Should Know About Mitt Romney.* Washington: Regnery Publishing, 2007.

Kantor, Jodi. "At Harvard, a Master's in Problem Solving." *New York Times,* December 24, 2011. http://www.nytimes.com/2011/12/25/us/politics/how-harvard-shaped-mitt-romney.html?_r=1&pagewanted=all.

Klein, Joe. "Why Don't They Like Mitt?" *Time,* December 1, 2011. http://swampland.time.com/2011/12/01/mitt-romney-why-dont-they-like-him/#ixzz1mq34Pps8.

Kranish, Michael and Scott Helman. "The Meaning of Mitt." *Vanity Fair,* February 2012. http://www.vanityfair.com/politics/2012/02/mitt-romney-201202.print.

"A Liberal, a Moderate and a Conservative Walk into a Bar." Sleepless in Midland, February 10, 2012. http://sleepless.blogs.com/george/2012/02/a-liberal-a-moderate-and-a-conservative-walk-into-a-bar.html.

Luo, Michael, and Michael Cooper. "Republican Candidates Put Bite Into a Debate, With Thompson a Target." *New York Times,* September 6, 2007. http://www.nytimes.com/2007/09/06/us/politics/06debate.html.

Martin, Jonathan. "Mitt Romney's Team Awaits 2012." Politico, June 29, 2009. http://www.politico.com/news/stories/0609/24316.html.

McElhenny, John. "Romney Sweeps to Victory." Boston.com, November 5, 2002. http://boston.com/news/daily/05/mass_gov.htm.

"'Meet the Press' transcript for June 28, 2009." MSNBC. http://www.msnbc.msn.com/id/31584983/ns/meet_the_press/t/meet-press-transcript-june/#.Tz0XXyPEOgs.

"Mitt Romney." 2012 Republican Candidates. http://2012.republican-candidates.org/Romney/Childhood.php.

"Mitt Romney Notable Quotes." America Needs Mitt. http://americaneedsmitt.com/blog/mitt-romney-resources/mitt-romney-notable-quotes/.

"Mitt Romney's Super Tuesday Victory Speech." Real Clear Politics. http://www.realclearpolitics.com/articles/2012/03/06/mitt_romneys_super_tuesday_victory_speech_113401.html.

Montopoli, Brian. "Following Disappointing Super Tuesday, Romney Considers His Options." CBS News, February 6, 2008. http://www.cbsnews.com/8301-502163_162-3798447-502163.html.

Nagourney, Adam and Marc Santora. "Republican Candidates Hold First Debate, Differing on Defining Party's Future." *New York Times,* May 4, 2007. http://query.nytimes.com/gst/fullpage.html?res=9C07EFDB113EF937A35756C0A9619C8B63&pagewanted=all.

Primack, Dan. "Newt Gingrich's Private Equity Past." CNNMoney, January 9, 2012. finance.fortune.cnn.com/2012/01/09/newt-gingrichs-private-equity-past/.

Radsken, Jill. "Ann Romney on Her Choices, Family, Health and Future." All About Multiple Sclerosis, from *Boston Herald,* December 8, 2002. http://www.mult-sclerosis.org/news/Dec2002/AnnRomney.html.

Riley, Charles. "What Mitt Romney Did at Bain." CNNMoney, January 10, 2012. http://money.cnn.com/2012/01/10/news/economy/romney_bain_capital/index.htm.

"Romney Attacks Obama in N.H. Victory Speech." Uploaded January 11, 2012. http://www.youtube.com/watch?v=VyNFF4KvqJo.

"Romney, Giuliani Spar During Thompson's Debate Debut." CNN, October 9, 2007. http://articles.cnn.com/2007-10-09/politics/thompson.debate_1_debate-debut-mitt-romney-watch-giuliani?_s=PM:POLITICS.

Romney, Mitt. *No Apology: The Case for American Greatness*. New York: St. Martin's Press, 2010.

_____. *The Real Romney*. New York: HarperCollins, 2012.

_____. *Turnaround: Crisis, Leadership, and the Olympic Games*. Washington: Regnery Publishing, 2007.

"Romney Second in N.H., but Pledges Long Fight." MSNBC, January 8, 2008. http://www.msnbc.msn.com/id/22563145/ns/politics-decision_08/t/romney-second-nh-pledges-long-fight/#.Tzf7VSPEOgs.

"Romney Takes Heat For RomneyCare From Santorum, Gingrich." Real Clear Politics, October 18, 2011. http://www.realclearpolitics.com/video/2011/10/18/romney_takes_heat_for_romneycare_by_santorum_gingrich.html.

"Romney's Michigan Win Shakes Up GOP Race." CNN, January 15, 2008. http://articles.cnn.com/2008-01-15/politics/michigan.primary_1_mike-huckabee-john-mccain-giuliani-campaign?_s=PM:POLITICS.

"Romney's New Message: I Care." Daily Kos, February 9, 2012. http://www.dailykos.com/story/2012/02/09/1063244/-Romney-s-New-Message-I-Care.

Roy, Avik. "What Mitt Romney Said About Romneycare When He Signed It into Law." *Forbes,* May 12, 2011. http://www.forbes.com/sites/aroy/2011/05/12/what-mitt-romney-said-about-romneycare-when-he-signed-it-into-law/.

Schultheis, Emily. "Santorum on Missouri, Minnesota: 'Conservatism is Alive and Well.'" Politico, February 7, 2012. http://www.politico.com/blogs/burns-haberman/2012/02/santorum-on-missouri-minnesota-conservatism-is-alive-113826.html.

Semuels, Alana. "Romney, An Active Man of Faith." *Los Angeles Times,* December 7, 2011. http://articles.latimes.com/2011/dec/07/nation/la-na-romney-faith-20111208.

"Spouses." 2012 Presidential Candidates. http://2012.presidential-candidates.org/Spouses.php.

Swidey, Neil and Michael Paulson. "Privilege, Tragedy, and a Young Leader." Boston.com, June 24, 2007. http://www.boston.com/news/nation/articles/2007/06/24/privilege_tragedy_and_a_young_leader/.

Tully, Shawn. "5 Painful Health-care Lessons from Massachusetts." CNNMoney, June 16, 2010. http://money.cnn.com/2010/06/15/news/economy/massachusetts_healthcare_reform.fortune/index.htm.

Tumulty, Karen. "Mitt Romney Florida Primary Win Puts Renewed Pressure on Gingrich." *Washington Post,* February 1, 2012. http://www.washingtonpost.com/politics/mitt-romney-florida-primary-win-puts-renewed-pressure-on-gingrich/2012/02/01/gIQA-4KO9hQ_story.html.

Vidmar, Tiger. *Behind the Mask: Mitt Romney.* Kee Mosabi Graphics, 2011.

Weiner, Eric. "GOP: McCain Leads Race for Delegates." NPR, February 6, 2008. http://www.npr.org/templates/story/story.php?storyId=18718573.

"What Romney Said in Stratham." *Concord Monitor,* June 2, 2011. http://www.concord-monitor.com/blogentry/260625/what-romney-said-in-stratham?SESS9834b15542a6fac1085e8e8200c5ec0c=google.

Web sites

www.mittromney.com

 The official campaign Web site of Mitt Romney

www.ontheissues.org

 Provides quotes and background on Romney on a
 range of issues, including gun control, civil rights,
 abortion, immigration, foreign policy, war and peace,
 the environment, and tax reform

Index

Photo Credits

All images used in this book that are not in the public domain are credited in the listing that follows:

2:	Courtesy of Paul Goyette
6-7:	Courtesy of BU Interactive News
9:	Courtesy of Jnn13
15:	Associated Press
16:	Associated Press
21:	Courtesy of the Special Collections Department, J. Willard Marriott Library, University of Utah.
27:	Bettman/Corbis/AP Images
28:	Associated Press
32:	Courtesy of National Archives and Records Administration
36-37:	Courtesy of U.S. Department of Agriculture
38:	Used under license from istockphoto.com
40:	Associated Press
44:	Associated Press
52-53:	Courtesy of Scott Catron
54:	Associated Press
56:	Associated Press
58:	Associated Press
62:	Courtesy of Ian Howard
64:	Associated Press
67:	Associated Press
70-71:	Associated Press
71:	Associated Press
74-75:	Associated Press
77:	Courtesy of Master Sargeant Cecilio Ricardo, U.S. Air Force
78:	Courtesy of Gage Skidmore
83:	Courtesy of Gage Skidmore
87:	Associated Press
90:	Jim West/Alamy
94-95:	Associated Press